MICHEL FOUCAULT

AN INTRODUCTION TO THE STUDY OF HIS THOUGHT

MICHEL FOUCAULT

AN INTRODUCTION TO THE STUDY OF HIS THOUGHT

BARRY COOPER

Studies in Religion and Society
Volume 2

The Edwin Mellen Press
New York and Toronto

Library of Congress Cataloging in Publication Data

Cooper, Barry, 1943-
    Michel Foucault, An Introduction to the Study
    of His Thought

    (Studies in Religion and Society; v.2)
    Bibliography: p.
    Includes index.
    1. Foucault, Michel.   I. Title.   II. Series:
    Studies in Religion and Society (New York, N.Y.);
    v.2
    B2430.F724C66   1982   194   82-8260
    ISBN   0-88946-867-2

Studies in Religion and Society   ISBN   0-88946-863-X

Printed in the United States of America

To S.P.

"Il n'est pas possible que le pouvoir s'exerce
sans savoir; il n'est pas possible que le
savoir n'engendre pas de pouvoir."

M. Foucault

MICHEL FOUCAULT:

AN INTRODUCTION TO THE STUDY OF HIS THOUGHT

INTRODUCTION

The power and energy of Michel Foucault's intellect are
as astounding as the range of topics on which he has written.
Ever since the popular success of *Les mots et les choses* in
1966 he has been in the public eye; after 1970, when he entered
the Collège de France, he became a certified man-of-letters,
called upon to express his views on all kinds of things. In
this role he has produced catalogues for art galleries, intro-
ductions to collections of cartoons, and a very large number
of prefaces. But even discounting this occasional material,
Foucault has written a great deal and has written it very
persuasively.

He has described his books as tool-boxes, and invited us
to make what use of them we may. In this essay I have accepted
his invitation and selected those hammers and screw-drivers
that are most useful for political science. Historians,
philosophers, literary critics would probably find other things
to attract their attention. Foucault is, after all, "Professor
of the History of Systems of Thought" and we are at liberty to
pillage his repertoire. The discussion approximately follows
the chronology of Foucault's own work. By way of introduction,
however, I will present a summary of his account of the configuration of recent history, and of the task of thought within
it.

THOUGHT AND MODERN DISCOURSE

1

In his lectures at the Collège de France, Foucault has
analyzed certain aspects of ancient,classical and medieval
culture. Most of his published work, however, has dealt with
what he has called the "classical period." The phrase, "l'âge
classique" indicates the century and a half prior to the French
Revolution. The next century and a half comprise the modern
age to which the present is discontinuously related. Period-
ization is not a vain exercise. It helps constitute meanings
in human life by announcing or making articulate patterns of
events. But pattern does not imply a smooth transition of
neatly-geared schedules, of the gradual sliding of one shape
into another. On the contrary, Foucault again and again has
emphasized discontinuity, phase-shifts, strophic transformations, and heterogeneity.

Every age, Nietzsche said, has a limit or horizon that
can be seen *as* horizon only when it has been transcended. One
transcends the limit of the age not by prolonging it in time,
not by continuing what is given, hoping that something surprising will turn up to relieve the weary world of its boring
regularity. On the contrary, one transcends by exposing the
basis, by seeing what are the conditions according to which
the age has been constituted as an age. According to Foucault,
philosophy, if anything, is a diagnostic. "To diagnose the
present is to say what the present is, to say how our present
differs from all that is not it, that is, from our past."[1]
He could write this genealogy of the present, quite clearly,
only from within a horizon that was not modern, whatever else
it may be. The modern age, or rather, its present disintegration,

can be understood by means of a retrospective analysis or,
if you like, a criticism, of its origins, formation, and
establishment. For Foucault this involves an analysis of
the systems of institutional power-knowledge, of *pouvoir-
savoir*. And, as a purely pragmatic and commonsensical matter,
by knowing the basis of modern institutions, one knows the
constraints they impose and at the same time one can begin to
escape those constraints and make sense of the efforts of our
contemporaries to do the same thing.

     Foucault's understanding of historical periodization was
formed by his study of psychology and literature, but also by
the interpretation of Hegel given by Jean Hyppolite.[2] The
great alternative to philosophers of Foucault's generation was
provided by Alexandre Kojève, who had stressed the logical
completeness of the system of science or wisdom. Wisdom was,
moreover, continuous with history because it was the completion
of it. Hyppolite, on the other hand, emphasized the intrinsic
heterogeneity of the historical contents of the system, the
actual picture-gallery of images of existence. Whether the two
interpretations can be reconciled on Hegelian or any other
grounds we need not at present enquire. When, however, Foucault
wrote that, "in philosophy, we are in the midst of trying to
find out what thought is without using the old categories, and
above all trying to emerge at last from that dialectic of
spirit that Hegel once defined," we should bear in mind that
the Hegel he was apparently rejecting was the completed Kojèvian
sage.[3] An important methodological implication is that accurate
descriptions enable the heterogeneity and discontinuity of human
existence to show itself. This is so regarding the chronological
divisions indicated earlier, classical, modern (or historical),
and post-modern (or post-historical).

     The earliest beginnings of the classical period are
indicated with the voyages of exploration, discovery, and
overseas trade that got underway during the sixteenth century.
One may say, then, that the term largely refered to that

transitional era between the Christian-feudal old regime and
the period of bourgeois capitalism. The intellectual characteristic of the classical age emphasized by Foucault was not
so much the mathematization of knowledge, though that was not
unimportant, but what might be called the "applied mathematics"
or epistemological engineering that placed things in empirical
categories and files, in a general and determinate grid or
table that presented itself as the immediate order of things.
It was, Foucault said, "a system of signs, a sort of general
and systematic taxonomy of things."[4] This taxonomy existed by
means of the power of discourse to constitute representations
of reality. In principle it was a-historic, and did not
"develop."

In contrast, the "modern" period, which extended from the
French Revolution until after the Second World War, understood,
and still nostalgically or anachronistically understands, itself almost entirely in terms of "history." The subject of
"history" was "man," who also was the object of study scrut-
inized by the human or social sciences. Once this object of
knowledge, namely man, was made visible, eschatalogical historical
dreams and speculations were freed from reliance on God and could
appear as a task to be achieved by man himself. "Man could
become freed of his alienations, freed of all determinations
of which he was not the author; thanks to this knowledge that
he had of himself, he could again become, or become for the
first time, master and possessor of himself. In other words,
man was made an object of knowledge so that man could become
the subject of his own freedom and his own existence."[5]
Unfortunately, the closer that man was investigated, the less
that could be found. The psychological probe of madness, for
example, revealed the unconscious, lacerated by its own forces
and compulsions that apparently had nothing to do with the
"human essence" or "freedom"--that is, with "man." The inco-
herence of the human sciences was obscured by the creation of
totalizing, teleological categories or "myths" that claimed to

summarize all human knowledge and action in an understanding of
the present. Nineteenth-century historicism has been, then,
correctly characterized as dialectical and humanist: dialectical
because of its dynamic drive, humanist because of its topical
contents, "man."

The third stage of this truncated series began around 1950.
It may be described as post-modern or post-historical, post-
humanist or post-anthropological. The great predecessor was
Nietzsche, who knew that the death of God also meant the death
of "man." Post-historical thought of a Nietzschean or Fou-
cauldian kind is non-dialectical in the nineteenth-century
sense. It is not, however, concerned with nature, as was the
non-dialectical thought of the classical age. "Its proper
object will be knowledge such that this thought will be in a
secondary position with regard to the entirety or general run
of specialized knowledges."[6] The proper topic of post-historical
thought is not the content of the great debates, which was
nothing more than the history of opinions, but the space of
knowledge that made them possible and within which they once
appeared. Foucault's concern for the conditions or rules
governing the formation of discourse, for the concepts used
to study those discourses, and for the theoretical options,
limits, and horizons that they display or express distinguishes
him from historians and accounts for his self-identification
as an "archeologist" and of his activity as "archeology," terms
that are certainly meant to indicate something other than
history.

To expose the conditions of possibility of modern discourse
is to question in a very radical way its self-understanding as
truth. This, too, Foucault learned from Nietzsche. Unlike so
many philosophers, Nietzsche came to philosophy not from
reflection on science or mathematics and not from theology,
but from philology, from an interrogation of language. His
studies of Greek texts were not academic exegeses, as the
attacks on them by academic exegetes showed so well. He sought

to interrogate existence and the basis of the world; he sought
to know who speaks in everything that was said. Thus, for
Nietzsche, philosophy was not speculation nor was it the theory
of a practice. "It is an activity directly engaged in the
world. Language and discourse do not reflect upon the world.
They are part of the world. But the world, in turn, has its
nervous system constituted by what is said in it."[7] Consequently, philosophy was inherently practical. This was not
because words could have consequences but because speech was
already a practice, because what was called truth was a
combination of two practices, a discursive one called theory
or philosophical speech or specialized knowledge or science,
and a non-discursive one called power. The meaning of post-
historical philosophy, the philosophy that Foucault practices,
has accordingly been changed. "It seems to me that philosophy
no longer exists today. Not that it has disappeared but that
it is dissipated in a vast number of different activities:
those of the logician, the linguistic analyst, the ethnologist,
the historian, the revolutionary, the political man--all can
be forms of philosophical activity. To be philosophical in
the nineteenth century, reflection questioned itself on the
conditions of possibility of objects; to be philosophical today
involves every activity that makes a new object appear for
specialized knowledge or for practice, whether this activity
involves mathematics, linguistics, ethnology or history."[8]
To write the history not of "thought" but of what contains
thought, what embodies thought, of everything within which
there exists thought, leads one not only to philosophy as it
is conventionally practiced but also to novels, to jurisprudence, to politics, to prisons, for there is thought "even
in an administrative system or a prison."[9] Correspondingly,
statements take on a quasi-material being when uttered. They
become objects of desire and of power, and are open to the
tumult of will.

    We shall return to the question of discursive practices,

power, and will. The genesis of these later formulations lay in Foucault's conviction of the importance of heterogeneity. This may be seen in his earliest studies.

HETEROGENEITY

2

Foucault entered the Ecole Normale Supérieure in 1946 to study philosophy. He also worked with Jean Delay "who introduced [him] to the world of madmen."[10] He taught classes in psychopathology at the ENS, and in 1954 published a curious little book, *Mental Illness and Personality*. The first part of the book is a straightforward account of the history of psychiatry, bristling with definitions and great names. The second part, which was replaced in a later edition, is an untidy melange of Marxism, Pavlov, and current Soviet psychological notions. There he argued for the primacy of organic pathology over mental pathology, of physiology over psychology and, presumably, of physics over everything.

The aim of the second edition, given a new title, *Mental Illness and Psychology,* was the reverse. Its argument, he said, was to show "that mental pathology requires methods of analysis different from those of organic pathology, and that it is only by an artifice of language that the same meaning can be attributed to 'illnesses of the body' and 'illnesses of the mind.' A unitary pathology using the same methods and concepts in the psychological and physiological domains is now purely mythical, even if the unity of body and mind is in the order of reality."[11] Foucault has consistently sought to avoid reducing the many to the one just as he has consistently interested himself in the artifice of language. So far as "mental illness" was concerned, the consciousness that a patient had of his condition was held to be strictly original. He recognizes his own anomaly and is aware that he is separate from the world, that his consciousness is unlike the consciousness of others. "His consciousness of the illness arises from

within the illness; it is anchored in it, and at the moment the
consciousness perceives the illness, it expresses it." What
was involved, therefore, was not the contrast of normal and
deviant but difference and the appearance of difference in
society. Accordingly, difference was not merely the absence
of the same or a lack of sameness. For a psychology and a
psychiatry that saw madness as deviance or as illness, there
was nothing for it to learn. Indeed, there was nothing for
it to encounter and nothing in madness to astonish. Strictly
speaking there was no relation to truth or untruth, meaning
or non-meaning in the pseudo-encounter of such a psychology
with madness because psychology approached its object fully
armed as the truth of the truth. "And when, in lightening
flashes and cries, [madness] reappears, as in Nerval or Artaud,
Nietzsche or Roussel, it is psychology that remains silent,
speechless, before this language that borrows the meaning of
its own kind from that tragic split, from that freedom that,
for contemporary man, only the existence of 'psychologists'
allows him to forget." Psychologists and psychiatrists were
apparently just technicians. They could intervene to modify
behaviour, but could not know what they did. Moreover, they
were not neutral or benevolent therapists, but practitioners
of a "moralizing sadism" that cloaked itself in the rhetoric
of philanthropy and liberation. In fact, it might better be
said "that all [psychiatric] knowledge is linked to the
essential forms of cruelty."[12] This linkage of cruelty,
sadism and the masks of language to the practice of truth
was an early formulation of the central concept of power-
knowledge.

A second study, also published in 1954, was more directly
concerned with heterogeneity. In a lengthy introduction to
Ludwig Binswanger's analysis of dreams, Foucault underlined
the autonomy of dream-consciousness. Dreams were not a
"rhapsody of images," as Freud had argued. Images were alterations of perception, an "as if" perception, whereas dreams

were imaginary experiences. They were cut off from perception
and the perceptual world and were constituted only from inside.[13]
Binswanger wrote less about dreams and existence than existence
as it appeared to itself and could be deciphered in the mode of
being of a dream. "The dream, like every imaginary experience,
is therefore a specific form of experience that does not lend
itself to being completely reconstituted by psychological
analysis and whose contents indicate man as a transcended
being. The imaginary is the sign of transcendence; the dream
is the experience of this transcendence under the sign of the
imaginary."[14] The dream world was therefore a world of its
own, not in the sense that it was a subjective experience
totally uncontrolled by the norms of objectivity, but that it
was constituted in an original mode. The reason why dreams
expressed profound human meanings was not because they deployed
fatal mechanisms of compulsion but because they brought to light
the basic freedom of human existence. When, through repetition,
we come to call our dreams destiny, this meant only that
existence had fallen into a determination that it had always
been free to accept. "To dream is not another way of having
the experience of another world; for the dreaming subject, it
is the radical way to have the experience of his own world.
And if at this point the experience is radical, it is because
existence does not seem to be of the world."[15] This not being
of the world was the imaginary mode of freedom in the world.
Accordingly, the dream was not the result of imagination but
its condition of possibility: dreaming was not a lively and
strong way of imagining, imagining was the intending of
oneself in the element of the dream, a self-conscious dream
for which dream-consciousness was its foundation. The dream
made visible the fundamental moment of freedom in the world
"when the movement of existence finds its division point between
images, where it is alienated into a pathological subjectivity,
and expression, where it is fulfilled in objective history."[16]
Whether actualized as fulfillment or alienation, freedom moved

from its imaginary mode to its worldly one; but the one cannot be reduced to the other nor made to evaporate as "just" a dream.

MADNESS AND SOCIAL ORDER

3

During the mid-1950s Foucault taught French in Uppsala, and acted as director of the French Institutes in Warsaw and Hamburg. He pursued his own studies of madness, this time in its pre-Cartesian form, publishing only a translation of Viktor von Weizaeker's *Der Gestaltkreis*.[17] In 1961 he presented his thesis, majesterial in the manner preserved only by the French. *Folie et déraison* indicated the continuing theme of heterogeneity. The sub-title, *Historie de la folie à l'âge classique* suggested the second discontinuity. As Foucault said in his preface, "in the history of madness, two events mark this [radical alteration in the language used to describe it] with a singular sharpness: 1657, the creation of the Hôpital général and the 'great confinement' of the poor, and 1794, when the chains were removed [from the madmen] at Bicêtre."[18] The usual interpretation was that the blind repression of an absolutist regime gave way to the liberating truths of psychiatric medicine. The story, however, was more complex, and its meaning more ambiguous.

Because he insisted upon that ambiguity and upon the shadows of power that sustained the bright light of medical truth, Foucault has not found favour with psychiatrists.[19] If madness were not simply mental illness, but a judgement of power of one mind over another the pristine therapeutic vocation of these medical practitioners would be fatally undermined. And, indeed, Foucault had already argued in *Mental Illness and Psychology* that "mental illness has its reality and value *qua* illness only within a culture that recognizes it as such."[20] Other cultures valued the madmen as holy, as full of divine or diabolical powers, for example.

But however conceived, the madman was other than ordinary. Madness, Foucault said, is nothing but the absence of production, the absence of an *oeuvre*.[21] In terms derived from Nietzsche, Foucault called the experience of madness "tragic," that is, it went beyond the limits of our culture. Or, as Shoshana Felman said, "in the final analysis, madness may be defined . . . as an act of resistance to interpretation." In any event, madness was not a stable object of disinterested knowledge whose history may easily be recovered and written up. It had a variable meaning that emerged from the opposition and interplay of reason and unreason. In this dialectic neither element was privileged, whatever the historical adventures of the pair may have been. And, as everyone knows, reasonable men have named unreasonable ones mad and locked them up in order to cure them. The history of madness and unreason, then, amounted to the story of the exclusion of one part of society by another. By casting his topic in that particular form, what Foucault implicitly wished us to consider is that knowledge, *savoir*, is not simply reasoned discourse, that knowledge might well *also* be expressed as mad "discourse" about the world.[23]

The institutions of exclusion were transmitted to the classical age in the form of lazarettos. Just as abandonment of lepers would ensure their salvation, so the abandonment of the mad would ensure theirs. The invariate form was: social exclusion leads to spiritual reintegration--of the lepers into the spiritual body of Christ, of the mad into another spiritual body, eventually the spiritual body of reasonable men. Alternatively, they might be sequestered in *Narrenschiffen,* ships of fools, where they actually lived out what for ordinary people was a symbolic voyage towards reason. "It is for the other world that the madman sets sail in his fool's boat; it is from the other world that he comes when he disembarks. The madman's voyage is at once a rigorous division and an absolute passage."[2] Or again, and equally symbolically, the madmen were kept between the inside world of culture and the outside world of nature--

locked up in the city gates. None of this treatment would have
been pleasant if one were among the unfortunate mad. But
Foucault's point was that madness had an integral meaning of
its own. And, in any event, a large number of madmen wandered
free, village idiots, forest-dwelling trolls and witches,
hermits and eccentrics by the sea.

    To be more specific, the mad replaced the lepers as the
presence of death in life. By their excessive freedom, the
madman showed that he did not care to prepare for the end of
days: the fool in his heart said there was no God. The tide
of madness showed the ordinary that, in fact, the end was near.
No longer was nothingness present only as pestilence and war:
the threat of death was replaced by the mockery of madness.
"The head that will become a skull is already empty. Madness
is the déja-là of death."[25] At the same time as expressing
the otherness that used to belong alone to the apocalyptic
symbols of death, the madman was other in his freedom, like
the beasts, and also in his fool's wisdom, a combination of
ultimate bliss and supreme punishment, of omnipotence and
damnation. Madness preserved its own meaning into the seventeenth century as romance (Don Quixote), as just punishment
(Lady Macbeth), as passion deprived of its object of love (Lear).
But these forms of madness, which appeared as tragic realities,
were transitional. Under the bright and rising sun of reason,
madness became illusion. "Forms remain, now transparent and
docile, forming a cortège, the inevitable procession of reason.
Madness has ceased to be--at the limits of the world, of man
and death--an eschatalogical figure; the darkness has dispersed
on which the eyes of madness were fixed and out of which the
forms of the impossible were born. Oblivion falls upon the
world navigated by the free slaves of the Ship of Fools.
Madness will no longer proceed from a point within the world
to a point beyond, on its strange voyage; it will never again
be that fugitive and absolute limit. Behold it moored now,
made fast among things and men. Retained and maintained. No

longer a ship but a hospital."[26]

Henceforth and until very recently the mad, whether
dangerous or not, were kept in their place. They embarked
nowhere but were confined by reason to the labours of truth.
By the second half of the seventeenth century, one percent of
Paris were incarcerated in the Hôpital général--a respectable
figure even by GULag standards. The Hôpital général was not
a "hospital" in the modern sense. Its purpose was not to cure
the sick but to confine the idle. As work was the lot of fallen
men, idleness was rebellion against God's word and indistinguish
able from madness. Accordingly, the Hôpital général contained
besides lunatics, also criminals, libertines, beggars, vagabonds, blasphemers, the debauched, spendthrift fathers and
prodigal sons, but also homosexuals and the poor. This collectio
of (to us) heterogeneous people all expressed unreason in their
lives and represented as well a danger to the mercantilist state
to religious order, and to the family. Sloth, not pride was
the original sin. "The asylum was substituted for the lazar
house in the geography of haunted places as in the landscape
of the moral universe. The old rites of excommunication were
revived, but in the world of production and commerce."[27]

Evidence of an increasingly atheist age, the poor were
no longer the symbolic passage of God in man's image but a
scandal to productivity, equivalent to lunatics who likewise
represented nothing transcendent. When all meaning was related
to labour, not God, to productive but transient bodies, not
unproductive but immortal souls, then could the community
condemn and segregate all forms of social uselessness. In
a parody of the final judgement of the Christian apocalypse,
they were banished into another world, or at least out of the
common sight of this one. Release could come only after one
had re-subscribed to the moral pact of society: morality
could be administered like trade. The republic of the respectable (if not of the good), armed with a warrant to enforce its
own virtues, or to remove those who were an affront and a

scandal (if not partisans of evil) was born deep within the
ancien régime. Morality, as every revolutionary bourgeois
would admit, had become the concern of the state and so of
the police.[28] From the start, therefore, asylums were such
useful instruments of social order that even the Revolution
only altered the form of admission.

Under the ancien régime, the *lettres de cachet de famille*
were used to confine the unreasonable. Contrary to what one
may have thought, their use was not confined to the higher
aristocracy. They were in general use throughout the population, with street-corner scribes available for hire by the
unlettered. These scribes would draw up the document, which
was full of stock phrases and read rather like a modern contract,
and the petitioner would hand it in to the local prefecture of
police. If acted upon, the individual named in it would be
hauled off to Bicêtre or the Salpêtrière. After the Revolution,
of course, *lettres de cachet* were discontinued. But not until
1838 was a suitable substitute found when, by law, medical and
administrative (that is, police) approval were both required
for committal. The grounds were that an individual was
"dangerous," first of all to himself, and then to others.
One should, perhaps, point out that being "dangerous" is
neither a sickness nor a crime.[29] Confinement of the uncon-
ventional, of the other, of the unreasonable, enforced by the
police and upheld by medical reason would, evidently, ensure
social happiness, the bourgeois substitute for salvation.

The mad, then, were not fit to be seen, at least not in
public. But what use is a scandal if not to be enjoyed? So
the mad could be viewed and the scandal could titillate. After
all, the excessive robustness of the mad betrayed their kinship
to animals. Like brutes they would respond only to brutality;
like brutes they could be put on show. But there was nothing
to be said *to* them, nor would one listen to them. One does
not, unless mad oneself, discuss worldly affairs with pigs
and monkeys; one carries on no conversations with goats and

ostriches. Every unreasonable gesture was endowed with sense
by the observer not the actor. Their incoherent expressions
were a confused amalgam of error and dream. With error, madness
shared non-truth; with the dream, it presented and expressed
by the show of image and hallucination. But unlike the dream
it affirmed (falsely affirmed) its images as truth (that is,
as error). Only reason could unmask the pretence. Reason
was not, therefore, meditative or theoretical, but activist,
technical and interventionist. If, for example, reason identified melancholia with immobility, the cure would be to induce
movement. One might cure melancholics by centrifuging them.
"Movement no longer aimed at restoring the invalid to the
truth of the outside world, but only at producing a series
of internal effects, purely mechanical and purely psychological . . . . Medicine was now content to regulate and to
punish, with means which once had served to exorcise sin, to
dissipate error in the restoration of madness to the world's
obvious truth."[30] As there was no difference between the
moral and the physical, one could scour the body in order
to purify the soul. Mediation between the mad and the sane,
or rather between reason and unreason, was by way of infernal
instruments and reason's monologue of experimental justification backed by power. The control of madness by means of
immobilizing the bodies of the mad, by submitting them to
what in other contexts is called torture, was a configuration
of power-knowledge in the classical period. But cruelty had
a theoretical side as well.

      In the *Encyclopédie*, under "Folie" one can read: "to
deviate from reason without knowing it, because one is deprived
of ideas, that is to be an imbecile; to deviate from reason
knowingly, but to regret it, because one is a slave to violent
passion, that is to be weak; but to deviate with confidence and
in the firm conviction that one is following it, that seems to
me to be what one calls being mad. At least such are those
unfortunates that are shut away, and who perhaps do not differ

from the remainder of men save because their madnesses are less
common and because they do not participate in the order of
society." Here was a curious and astonishingly frank, not to
say cynical, text. To be mad was not simply to be blind, but
to be blind to blindness, to have the illusion of being
reasonable. But this made madness, too, a form of reason
or rather, of knowledge, and placed the danger and suspicion
of madness at the heart of reason. Both unreason and reason
would seem to be provinces of knowledge where each could
over-reach the other and denounce it as other. But this
unsettling implication was shoved out of sight with the
observation that, even if the mad were not so different from
the sane (whose madnesses are common rather than rare), still
good order demanded they be locked away. And good order was
called reason. Further on in the article this was made
explicit.

Madness must be seen in light of its contrary, reason.
And reason "is no other thing in general than knowledge of
truth" where truth was "sensible" and "available to all men."
They had the faculty of knowing because it was necessary to
them, either for the conservation of their being, for their
own particular happiness, or for the well-being of society.
Truth may be physical or moral. Physical truth was seeing
what others see. Hence, Don Quixote was mad. Moral truth
consisted in justice. "That a man commit a criminal action
in complete awareness of what he is doing, that is to be
wicked; that he do it and is persuaded it is just, that is to
be mad . . . . Every excess is madness, even of laudable
sentiments. Friendship, disinterestedness, love of glory,
all are laudible sentiments, but reason must give them limits;
it is madness to sacrifice to them, without necessity,
reputation, fortune and happiness . . . . There are no true
goods on earth besides health, freedom and moderation of
desires. Thus it is madness of the first order to sacrifice
involuntarily such great goods." There was nothing sacred or

tragic in madness since nothing had been lost. The mad saw
things differently and therefore could not take part in
(reasonable) society. Shut them away and social order, without
excess and rich in the moderation of its desires, would be
served and preserved.

From the brutalities of the Hôpital général to the vulgar
apology for social repression in the *Encyclopédie* was a short
step. Insulated behind the enlightened intellectuals was the
angelic and imperious Cartesian cogito, muttering to itself:
"I think, therefore, I am not mad; I am not mad, therefore I
am."[31]   For the age of such reason, madness was non-being,
and confinement, which followed logically, was the suppression
of the appearance of non-being. To the extent it was successful
the truth of reason would apparently be confirmed.

When, in 1794, Pinel had the madmen of Bicêtre released
from their chains, psychiatry, a new and thoroughly modern
science, was born. Modernity modified the pattern of classical
power-knowledge; it did not abolish it. In place of the
Cartesian simplicity that contrasted being and non-being, a
tripartite anthropological and organic model was substituted.
There exists "man," his disease, called madness, and its cure,
which was the province of a specialized science. Iron manacles
were heavy and inefficient; they could not cure a disease. The
newer, mind-forged models would do the job by using the fear
that the madman induced in the ordinary to purge him of unhealth.
The asylum would organize guilt on the model of the family, not
punish it. It would show the madman reason in his own conscience
and gradually constrain him gently to responsibility and self-
control. Once norms had been internalized, the shackles of
physical control would not be needed. The technology mobilized against mental disease would defeat unreason by words,
and the madman would become an object for himself, a being
who understood that he was constantly under judgement, the

paternal judgement of his own sovereign reason and logical
discourse. In other words, the asylum operated as a juridi-
cial not a therapeutic institution that happened to have
medically (not legally) qualified persons as judges.

A change in the perception of madness between the
classical and the modern period also led to a change in
treatment. When madness was seen as a form of error or
illusion, as an element in the realm of imagination, it
could be overcome, if at all, only by a massive exposure
to truth. Truth was not found in the artificial space of
the hospital, which served only to confine, but in nature,
the source of "normality." Long walks in the countryside,
repose among the peasantry, travel, those were the ways to
overwhelm illusion. Alternatively, there was the theatre,
the reversal of nature, where the madman would enact his
own madness, recognize that he was acting what he was, and
seeing the truth so displayed, overcome his errors. Such
"therapies," of course, were restricted to the small number
of madmen able to afford economically this expensive exposure
to truth. Most languished with the criminals and the poor.
When the modern perception of madness judged it not with
reference to truth but to normality, it appeared not as
disturbed judgement but as a difficulty in acting, willing,
controlling passions and making free decisions. "In short,
it was no longer inscribed on the axis truth-error-conscious-
ness, but on the axis passion-will-freedom."[32] The sickness
would be cured when, willy nilly, the patient behaved normally.

Several additional alterations in the configuration of
power-knowledge were implied by the medical treatment of
unreason. The construction of asylums, which resembled
hospitals, aided psychiatry in establishing its public
appearance as a branch of medicine. But asylums also looked
like prisons, which served to manifest the omnipresent danger
of madness and advertise the psychiatrists' claim that only
they stood between the madmen within the society without.

And inside, the asylum did function in part at least as a
hospital: it was the locale of diagnosis, classification,
and the accumulation of knowledge. Chiefly, however, it was
a space of confrontation: "madness, disturbed will, and
perverted passions must encounter in asylums correct will
and orthodox passions."[33] The doctor was the incarnation
of that will: his will eventually would overpower the sick
will of the patient. This double function of the asylums
sustained the double role of the psychiatrist. The great
psychiatrists of the nineteenth century could both "enunciate
the truth of illness by the knowledge that [they] had over
it" and they could "produce the illness in its truth and
submit it to reality by means of the power that [their] will
exercised over the sick person himself."[34] All the techniques
of nineteenth-century psychiatry--cold showers, moralistic
lectures, forced labour, rewards and punishments of all
sorts--had the purpose of making the psychiatrist master
not over the patient but over madness. The psychiatric doctor
would force madness into the open, make it appear in its true
form, and then would dominate it, calm it, cure it from within.
To say the least this exalted the power of the psychiatrist
and elevated his personality as the instrument of that power.
Charcot, for example, evidently had quasi-thaumaturgical
powers and could cure hysteria by touch. Less spectacular,
but more important, the power of psychiatric medicine was
justified by the awareness it produced a knowledge whose
general legitimacy was enhanced insofar as it could be
integrated into other branches of medical knowledge.

   The social justification of asylums expressed the
conjunction of power and knowledge even more explicitly.
As it happened, there was a marvellous harmony between the
requirements of public order, which had to be protected against
the disorder of the lunatics, and the necessities of therapy,
which required their isolation. Esquirol, perhaps the most
important French psychiatrist of the nineteenth century,

justified the isolation of madmen for the following reasons:
it would provide them with personal security and provide
security to their families; it would free them from external
influences; it would subdue any personal or idiosyncratic
resistance; it would force them to submit to a medical regime;
it would enable new intellectual and moral habits to be imposed.
That is, everything had to do with power: overcome the madman's power, neutralize external powers, establish therapeutic power. "Power-relations constitute the *apriori* of
psychiatric practice: they condition the functioning of
institutional asylums, they distribute relations between
individuals, they regulate the forms of medical intervention."[35]
The right of reason to exercise power over unreason, of
psychiatrists to "treat" madmen, was transcribed in terms
of competence over ignorance, of commonsense and access to
reality as a corrective to the errors of illusion, hallucination and fantasy, and of the need for normality to be imposed
on disorder and deviation. "It is this triple power that
constitutes madness as an object of possible knowledge for
medical science, that constitutes it as a sickness at the
very moment when the 'subject' contracting this sickness
finds himself disqualified because he is a madman, that is,
deprived of all power and of all knowledge concerning his
own sickness."[36]

If only the extremely disordered had to be committed
for treatment, this meant that the less disordered were
allowed to go free, to make up society. As in the *Encyclopédie,* their madness was more common; but unlike the
encyclopédiste this was not an ironical reflection, a back-
handed admission that something was amiss in the arro-
gations of reason. The nineteenth-century alienist drew the
more straightforward conclusion: he was more than a medical
doctor. Like the practitioners of that other new science,
sociology, his role was to defend the whole of society, to
uphold the entire social order. Psychiatry, then, was tied

to post-revolutionary industrializing, urbanizing society and
to its search for a spiritual and political order to replace
the dissolved alliance of throne and altar. "It is integrated into an entire strategy of regularity, or normalization, of assistance, of placing children, delinquents,
vagrants, the poor, and lastly and above all, the workers,
into a tutelary state where they can be watched."[37] The
psychiatrists were the cutting edge of public hygiene. The
therapies they imposed through punishment, re-education,
and moralization in the asylums were the practice of a
small-scale despotic utopia whose scientific success justified the claims of psychiatry to intervene permanently
on a broader but less severe scale in the order of society.[38]

The power of psychiatry today has hardly been diminished
from the golden age of the alienist. Everyone has become
potentially an object of psychiatric help: so subtle are
the ways of unreason that epidemics of madness may overwhelm us all before we know it. This is obvious if one
raises the question of how to get rid of asylums. Respectable opinion still answers: they are indispensible. There
do exist, however, the highly unrespectable opinions of
anti-psychiatry.

Psychiatry, from the start, has been traversed by a
questioning of the role of the psychiatrist as a producer of
truth within the confines of the hospital. De-psychiatrization probably began when it was suspected that the doctors
produced, rather than brought from darkness into light, the
crises of hysteria that they described, much as Pasteur
discovered that doctors transmitted many of the diseases
they were supposed to cure. In any event, the great crises
of nineteenth-century psychiatry called into question the
power of the doctor far more often than his knowledge or
the truth he pronounced over the patient. One means of

dealing with the problem was to make psychiatry more precise
and scientific. The theatrical role of the doctor could be
reduced by simplifying the process of curing: illness was
physical, and knowledge of its nature would allow for the
direct suppression of its manifestations. The result was
psycho-surgery, psycho- or neuro-pharmacology.[39] A second
criticism was exactly the opposite: the doctor should not
be trapped by the sovereign mechanisms he has produced with
his knowledge. Instead, a discursive freedom should mediate
the doctor-patient couple. Eventually this led to psychoanalysis. But both of those forms of de-psychiatrization
maintained the power of the doctor. The first, by annuling
entirely the question of truth, initiated an unbounded movement of technological self-augmentation; Freud, in contrast,
maintained in a refined and transposed way, all the structures
of the asylum that joined truth and power.[40] Anti-psychiatry
was and is opposed to these options because they both maintained intact the armature of power-knowledge. Rather than
continue the practice of power outside the asylum, as did
psycho-analysis, anti-psychiatry sought the destruction or
self-destruction of the asylum. Transference would be not to
the doctor, as in psychoanalysis, but to the patient who then
could gain the power of producing his own madness and the
truth of his own madness, rather than have it reduced to zero,
as is the objective of the immoderate technicians. Anti-
psychiatry, with which Foucault is in great sympathy, had
nothing to do with the truth of psychiatry in terms of a
specialized knowledge because such knowledge must always be
bound up with power. Anti-psychiatry sought to remove the
element of power-knowledge by refusing to judge madness as
a mental illness or a pathology. That is, it sought to
de-medicalize madness. So far as any concrete proposals go
however, Foucault has made the obvious response: "my position
is not to propose. The moment one 'proposes' then one proposes
a vocabulary and an ideology that can only result in domin-

ation."[41] It was enough to present analyses of the discourses of the functionaries of social order.

Anti-psychiatry introduced the further and more difficult question, namely the relationship between madness and specialized knowledge of it, which was *the* form of power-knowledge: "is it possible that the production of the truth of madness could be achieved by forms that are not related to knowledge?"[42] This is, in fact, an enormous problem: how can one say what is other without transforming it to a moment of one's own speech, that is, to an element of the same, in this case, reason. How, that is, can reason interrogate unreason save by demanding that unreason answer its questions, which is to say, become reasonable and thereby cease to be what it is. There is, in other words, a built-in bias in language that it be reasonable, which therefore disqualified it from interrogating unreason. Unreason does not question the affirmations of reason, reason does. Unreason has its own work to do, someplace else, away from here, constantly on the go to wherever that elsewhere is--or is not. That was why Foucault called it an absence of an *oeuvre*. And yet, unreason could appear, as Foucault said, in the literary production of authors such as Nerval and Artaud, Hölderlin, Nietzsche or Roussel. There it appeared in all its power, the equal of reasoned discourse: no one but a mad psychiatrist would think he could understand Hölderlin or Nietzsche by subjecting them to the ministrations of medical power.[43]

LANGUAGE

4

   Reduced by the technicians of reason first to infantil-
ism and then to silence, unreason expressed itself in violence,
in politics, in art, and especially in literature. "Through
Sade and Goya, the western world received the possibility of
transcending its reason in violence, and recovering tragic
experience beyond the promises of dialectic."[44] Madness in
art and the paradoxically articulate unreason of literature
opened up a silence, a void in the texture of the world and,
through the expression and, indeed, the being of transgression,
forced the everyday to question itself. Nothing guaranteed in
advance that the world was justified by the works of unreason
that judged it. One can say, however, that this literary
buffer between the uncontrolled discourse of unreason and the
complete control of reason could express the unthought residue
of thought. It could do so not, obviously, through the
imposition of conceptual precision but in the mode of participation. The recovery of tragic experience that Foucault
mentioned must be undertaken from within: one must participate in it and not merely talk about it. Just as Nietzsche
argued that the tragic structure from which the history of
the west has proceeded was the result of the refusal to
countenance, and so, to suppress or "forget," tragedy through
history, so Foucault argued that the echoes and residues of
unreason still dimly present even in the technician's madness
proceeded from the logical, rational and historical refusal,
suppression and "forgetting" of unreason.
   Literature was the privileged medium for articulate
unreason. In common with unreason, it did not speak according

to a pre-established code but developed its own internal
discourse (or not) as it proceeded. It must be decyphered,
which is to say, re-stated in terms more directly accessible
to reason. Its imaginative words were not simply the presence
of a pre-existing linguistic medium but created their own
sense when they were uttered. It is not surprising, then,
that much of the best informed commentary on Foucault's work
has been done by literary critics or more generally, by students
of language. Foucault himself said that literary works,
especially Maurice Blanchot and Raymond Roussel were important
influences on the argument of *Folie et déraison*. "What interested and guided me," he said "was a certain presence of
madness in literature."[45] He has, moreover, reflected at
length on his own discourse about previous discourse and has
defined his world in terms of language: "we live in a world
of signs and of language and that, I think, is precisely the
problem . . . a number of us, I think, including myself,
consider that reality does not exist, that only language
exists and what we talk about is language; we talk within
language, and so on."[46] Much of his work in the 1960s was
in the realm of what is conventionally called literary
criticism.[47] The importance Foucault attributed to language
is perhaps best indicated in his book on Raymond Roussel.

Roussel was a peculiar stylist and a peculiar individual.
He was born in 1877 into a wealthy family extensively connected
with the aristocracy of the first Empire. His father, a
successful stockbroker, died young and he was raised by his
mother, an eccentric patron of the arts. He was under the
psychiatric care of Pierre Janet for some time and died in
1933, in Palermo, after several weeks of a drug-induced
euphoria. In a 6000-line verse-novel, *La Doublure* (1897),
he proclaimed himself the equal of Dante and Shakespeare.
This work went largely unnoticed. In 1907 he created a
technique or "chiffre" for composition. Based on the extensive use of dictionaries, it combined random association and

poetic imagination. He called it "verbal procedure" or
"evolving procedure," and used it to write a number of plays,
all of which were greeted with tumultuous hostility save for
the applause of the surrealists whose esteem Roussel did not
reciprocate. His reasons became clear with a posthumous publication that explained the "secrets" of his writing, *Comment
j'ai écrit certains de mes livres*.

A few examples may make it clear that something needs to
be explained. One "procedure" consisted in repeating the
opening phrase of a story at its end with a change of but
one letter or sound to produce an entirely different meaning.
The second story of *Comment j'ai écrit* began: "les anneaux
du gros serpent à sonnettes," which means "the coils of the
large rattlesnake." The concluding phrase was: "les anneaux
du gros serpent à sonnets," which means "a pair of ear-rings
given to the narrator, who had saved him from a boa constrictor
(not a rattlesnake), by a big man who writes sonnets and plays
a brass instrument known as a serpent." In another story, a
Roman chariot, "char," whose wheels, rather like Red River
carts, gave out a screech at high "C,", "qu'ut y est," began
its existence as a pork-butcher, "charcutier," which also
means surgeon. In his plays Roussel would take two nouns,
each having more than one meaning, which he would link with
"à." Hence the reaction to them--as if the works of Shakespeare and Dante were a series of puns, many of which were
strained or unintelligible without a *Grand Larousse*. One
commentator observed that Roussel scholarship demands a taste
for crossword puzzles and treasure hunting as much as anything else.

Foucault would not disagree, though unlike commonsense
scholarship he saw more in Roussel than an imaginative oddity.
In the story of the large rattlesnake and the serpent-playing
sonnet-writer, for example, *both* phrases were artificial. It
was impossible to say which was the original and which the
variant. Precisely the point, according to Foucault. Words

in the present world are exceedingly unreliable: similar words
may signify dissimilar things, the same word may signify
entirely different things. All one can do is consult the
text and accept the gaps it contains. Roussel's technique,
in fact, revealed the abyss in the picture of reality that
words ordinarily concealed. Foucault found it very significant that Roussel deliberately arranged things so that he would
be found dead, on the threshold of a locked door (the first
chapter of Foucault's study was called "le seuil et la clef").
That is, there were gestures that signified nothing beyond
themselves, that were at once riddled with emptiness (drug
euphoria and death) and were the expressions of it (the door
to the adjoining apartment of his lover was locked; the door
to the common hallway was not). In Foucault's words, "this
gap, like all those found in Roussel, contains within its
symmetrical parentheses a circle of words and things that is
born from itself, that completes its own movement within a
self-sufficiency so that nothing external can disturb its
purity and enclosed glory, so that it ends up in a repetition
that, whether it is fated from the start or the consequence
of a sovereign will, ends up in the disappearance of itself."[48]
Roussel's technique, which combined the most outrageous con-
tingencies, resulted in an immobile text whose movements were
all internal, all fixed in advance according to the machinery
of its composition. "Nothing is displaced; everything sings
the perfection of a repose that vibrates upon itself, where
each figure slides around only the better to indicate its
own place and at once to return to it."[49] In other words,
the combination of chance and necessity in Roussel's poems
effected an abolition of time and movement by the circularity
of its linguistic space. Likewise, his minute description,
at great length, of the picture on the label on a bottle of
Evian mineral water was intended to demonstrate the independence of words from natural bodily space. There are at
present no "natural" perspectives so far as words are

concerned. Words and things are now joined, if at all, by history and thus by conventions. And conventions have always been discontinuous.

Roussel, then, was more than a pun-smith. What he attempted to do was express the tie that language makes between the visible surface of things in "ordinary" space and time, and their invisible meaning. "It is there, between what is hidden in the manifest and luminous in the inaccessible that is lodged the task of his language . . . . His language shows that the visible and the non-visible are infinitely repeated and that this redoubling of the same gives language its sign: what makes it possible to have its origin among things and what makes it possible for things to be what they are only through language."[50] He explored the ambiguous realm where words hit and miss things, "that empty and mobile space where words glance off things," where things and words designated one another but also hid and betrayed one another. In his later work Merleau-Ponty used an equally strange language, derived from painting, to describe this realm where words meant and did not mean what they did.

In addition, Roussel (like Artaud, whom Foucault often mentioned in the same context) was directly in touch with unreason, even while making it explicit and therefore part of the world of discourse. Indeed, one may say that the peculiarities of Roussel's discourse came from the demand he made that it express its own self-cancellation. The result was "absurd." And now, today, there is an entire "literature of the absurd" that is quite unreasonable, quite out of touch with the world--"mad" even--but not without meaning. "We understand that it is not 'meaning' that is missing, but signs which signify, however, only by not being there. In this confused play of existence and history, we simply discover the general law of the Play of Signs within which our reasonable history is played out." Roussel initiated a literary language into a strange and uncanny space. He

invented a language "that says only itself, an absolutely
simple language in its being redoubled, a language of language, enclosing its own sun within its own sovereign and
central extinction . . . . The anxiety of the signifying,
that is what makes Roussel's efforts the solitary expression
of what is closest to us in our own language. What makes
the illness of this man our problem. And what allows us to
speak of him on the basis of his own language."[51] What
Foucault said of Roussel may be said equally of him:
Foucault's language compels one to enter a strange world
of power and desire, of fear, violence, and pleasure, of
transgression, madness, and absence. It is a wierd language
but it should not for that reason be dismissed, as it has been,
as poetic necromancy. Rather, it serves to bring those dark
realities into light so we can see them and be touched by
them for what they are. He has described some of those in-
timations of deprival that George Grant has told us are
precious.

THE CLINICAL GAZE

5

In his early work, Foucault centred his reflections on the heterogeneity of human experience. Heterogeneity, discontinuity, disjunction were not, evidently, easy to accept. In them modern reason found a threat and was imperious enough to seek to reduce the manifold of reality to its own continuous, logical, and homogeneous categories. The process of transformation was not theoretical but practical, an act backed by power and made effective by power. This was evident from the history of madness, though it was not the object of an explicit analysis. The study of Roussel and the other "absurd" writers showed what happened to unreason when the attempt was made, through medical technology, to stifle into silence its incoherent voice. Moreover, literature introduced the topic of language and its relationship to "things," which was the subject of Foucault's most famous book, and which prompted him to reflect explicitly on methodological questions connected with his work. These are discussed in the next section. In *Naissance de la clinique,* published the same year as the book on Roussel, Foucault discussed in great detail one of the most important forces of modern and contemporary social and political homogenization.

"This book," Foucault announced in the preface, "is about space, about language, and about death; it is about the act of seeing, the gaze."[52] The link with *Folie et déraison* was obvious enough: the first dealt with souls and the second with bodies. But both were concerned with the power of discourse to influence the affairs of human beings by altering the terms of their self-understanding. In the earlier book Foucault insisted one must look to the time

when reason and unreason had not dissociated one from another;
in *The Birth of the Clinic* "we must look beyond the thematic
content [of language] or its logical modalities to the region
where 'things' and 'words' have not yet separated and where--
at the most fundamental level of language--seeing and saying
are still one."[53]   That is, once again, the change between
the classical age and the modern was under investigation,
only this time with reference to the relationship between
the visible and the invisible in medical perception.

Everyone can be persuaded to admit that there is a large
difference between a treatise on the art of medicine written
in 1780 and one on pathological anatomy written in 1820.   For
the heirs of Descartes and Malebranche, to see was to perceive.
What was involved was rendering the body transparent for the
exercise of thought.   The shadows of obscurity were to be
reduced and removed by the light of the mind.   At the end of
the eighteenth century, seeing meant leaving the density and
opacity of things closed upon themselves and allowing the
slow and deliberate passage of the gaze to fix individual
things objectively so as to organize rational language around
them.   "This new structure is indicated . . . by the minute
but decisive change, whereby the question 'what is the matter
with you?' with which the eighteenth-century dialogue between
doctor and patient began, . . . was replaced by that other
question: 'where does it hurt?' in which we can recognize
the operation of the clinic and the principle of its entire
discourse."[54]   The change, that is, was from a dialogue that
began in a lecture hall and that aimed to decypher to an
expert examination undertaken and undergone in a clinic.   The
objective of *The Birth of the Clinic,* which was made even
more explicit in *Les Mots et les choses,* was to disentangle
the conditions of the history of this discourse from the
actual density of the discourse itself.   "My problem ,"
Foucault has said, "was to know what were the groups of
necessary and sufficient transformations within the regime

of discourse itself so that one could employ one set of words
rather than another, one type of analysis rather than another,
how one could look at things from one angle and not from
another."[55] What counts in such analysis was not what the
authors may have thought about the things they said but
what systematized their words and made them accessible to
other transformative discourses. It was also what ensured
that the consequences of those discourses would be integrated
with the words themselves. In order to do this, one must read
a great deal; in principle, one must read everything.[56]

In the classical period, disease, life, and nature were
linked. Diseases were simple among the simple people, more
complex among the frantic inhabitants of large cities.
"Peasants and workers still remain close to the basic
nosological table; the simplicity of their lives allows it
to show through in its reasonable order: they have none of
those variable, complex, intermingled nervous ills, but
down-to-earth apoplexies or uncomplicated attacks of mania."[57]
Even more than nervous ills, bodily ones were best dealt with
in the natural locus of life, the family. The environment of
affection and care would gently assist nature in its struggle
against illness. The hospital, in contrast, was a place where
diseases grew complex and distorted. Besides, they were
unproductive and endowed in perpetuity, which was an invitation
to waste.

A new era, which eventually would economize the function
of hospitals, was begun with a new question: what is an
epidemic? Not the act of a wrathful God, but a qualitatively
large disease. And, of course, the equation could be reversed:
what was sporadic disease but a submarginal epidemic? The
political importance of epidemics was obvious. But epidemi-
ology also changed the social position of doctors, since they
were in charge of discovering and then combatting disease.
The prestige and power of doctors was clearly tied to the
State. "A medicine of epidemics could exist only if supple-

mented by a police: to supervise the location of mines and
cemeteries, to get as many corpses as possible cremated
instead of buried, to control the sale of bread, wine, and
meat, to supervise the running of abattoirs and dye works,
and to prohibit unhealthy housing."[58] Eighteenth-century
medicine and its contemporary successor developed, therefore, in a two-dimensional process. On the one hand was
the medicine of the "free market" centred upon clinical
examination and individual therapy that endowed the doctor
with moral and scientific authority. Second, however, the
intervention of the state introduced a politics of health
and disease. That is, sickness was seen to be an economic
and political problem requiring action by the collectivity.
Private and socialized medicine were not, therefore, simply
opposed to one another but, historically existed in combination and even today constitute a global strategy that
includes opposition within a more general reciprocity. We
consider explicity the question of the politics of health
below.

     In the present context it is enough to note that the
state was called upon to provide a new legal definition of
a physician that was neither a restoration of the corpor-
atism of the old regime nor simply the creation of a new
branch of police. The principle of organization sought to
ensure that doctors were competent, knowledgeable, experienced, and the embodiment of "recognized probity." The
doctor, that is, was seen as the "normative agent of social
space,"[59] the curate of bodies and heir to the priest. In
the midst of the household the physician appeared as *the*
figure of authority. With his presence came an ethic of
self-discipline and self-regulation, in the absence of which
one would surely fall ill--*he* said. So it was accepted that
it was impossible to live without doctors, men who appeared
in the form of servants but, wrapped in the dignity of truth,
could legitimately claim the authority and the nobility of

power. The free gaze of the doctor, which sought only to discover what disease was there already, received from that claim the right to destroy. His look was purified by being invested with knowledge and it sought the purification of the sick. Freed from darkness himself, the doctor could dissipate darkness while adding none of his own. Once, that is, that medicine had become a public, disinterested, and supervised activity, the alleviation of physical misery was, indeed, close to the spiritual vocation of the Church.

The pay was better, of course, and so were the rewards of power. Physical misery was not just disease, nor were diseases uncaused. Physicians soon saw their role as the production of health, not merely the curing of unhealth. This required knowledge of the non-sick, of model individuals and of norms that, in turn, opened up a potential space of opportunity into which physicians could act. Thus was born the dream of a healthy society, a society freed of sickness, freed of abnormality, and bursting with moral vitality. And the doctor, who knew what health was, was the key advisor to the legislator. Progress in industry, then, formed a bond, which has not yet been broken, with medicine in the broad sense of the term, that is, with public hygiene, with the science of mental illness, with the science of crime, and all the institutions of social assistance as well as of social repression.

The politicization of medicine was made effective by establishing grids of detection. There would exist, in a healthy society, a generalized medical presence made up of doctors whose intersecting and overlapping observations would form a network of differentiated but constant and mobile supervision. It was not humanitarianism that brought medical services to the countryside but the political consequences of epidemics and the desire of medicine to establish a regime of supervised normalcy. This medical field was similar in its geometry to the social space dreamed of by the original men of '89: "a form homogeneous in each of its regions, constituting a set of equivalent items capable of maintaining constant relations with their entirety, a space of free communication in which the relationship of the parts to the whole was always transposable and reversible. There is, therefore, a spontaneous and deeply rooted convergence between the requirements of political ideology and those of medical technology."[60] Implied, that is, in the organization of public health was an undivided domain, scanned from top to bottom by an expert and omnipresent gaze.

There is no action without disturbance, and the creation of a medical network had its own costs to pay. Merely examining in order to know, showing in order to teach or learn, involved "a tacit form of violence, all the more abusive for its silence upon a sick body that demands to be comforted, not displayed. Can pain be a spectacle? Not only can it be, but it must be, by virtue of a subtle right that resides in the fact that no one is alone, the poor man no less so than others, since he can obtain assistance only through the mediation of the rich."[61] The equivalence of sick bodies for the clinical gaze was contradicted by differing material circumstances. The hospital provided a means of economic resolution. "The hospital became viable for private initiative from the moment that sickness, which had come to seek a cure, was turned into a spectacle."[62] Thanks to the virtues of the clinical gaze, the poor, by providing information, paid the interest on the capital that the rich had consented to invest in hospital construction and maintenance.

Tacitly violent, the clinical gaze was inherently technical. The illumination of obscurities, the slow and prudent reading of appearance, the patient calculation of risk, all had as its objective not the observation of an individual but the collection of a dossier of facts. "The mathematical model is always explicit and invoked; it is

present as the principle of coherence of a conceptual process
that culminates outside itself; it is a question of the
contribution of themes of formalization."[63] Facts, mathematical
formality and statistical frequency spelled an end to the
natural family environment as a contribution to curing.
Medical knowledge would do it alone, within "a neutral domain,
one that is homogeneous in all its parts and in which comparison is possible and open to any form of pathological event,
with no principle of selection or exclusion."[64] What was
there could be made wholly visible and could be completely
expressed. Disease became a series of specifiable accidents,
practically infinite in number, but capable of being controlled by the gaze that broke them into factual units and
constituted these simplicities into enduring wholes. But
not everyone could see what was there. Not that healing was
a mysterious art into whose secrets one had to be initiated,
but that training in the techniques of truth was not univer-
sally available. Accordingly a new hierarchy and a new
esotericism was constituted. It was far removed from the
Latin of the old physicians, whose language served simply
to exclude and preserve corporate privileges. "Now operational
mastery over things is sought by accurate syntactic usage and
a difficult semantic familiarity with language."[65] Description
in clinical medicine was true speech within a homogeneous
technical field.

The greatest appearance of homogeneity in the world is
the act by which we all appear in it, and more importantly,
the act by which we leave it. Not surprisingly, therefore,
pathological anatomy grew increasingly important as a source
of knowledge. Prior to the eighteenth century it was carried
out in great fear of the dead; with the enlightenment, death,
too, was entitled to the clear light of reason and was
rendered capable of becoming a source of knowledge. Corpses
made things clear: "the knowledge of the living, ambiguous
disease could be aligned upon the white visibility of the

dead."[66] No longer content with symptomatic surfaces, the
gaze must also look inside. Opening up corpses was how to
do it. The institution of the clinic was in this regard
absolutely necessary. If the traces of disease also consumed
the body, then it would be difficult to distinguish between
the effects of disease and the ordinary decay that followed
death. Pathological anatomy, the technology of the corpse,
could provide a more rigorous and instrumental status to
disease as well as a conceptual mastery of death only if the
period between death and autopsy were reduced to a minimum
so that "the last stage of pathological time and the first
stage of cadaveric time almost coincide."[67] Death, the
great homogenizer, was represented conceptually as a vertical,
absolutely thin line, a membrane that joined by dividing the
series of symptoms and the series of lesions. Only in death
could one see clearly and analyze organic dependencies and
pathological sequences. "Instead of being what it so long
had been, the night in which life disappeared, in which even
the disease becomes blurred, it is now endowed with that
great power of elucidation that dominates and reveals both
the space of the organism and the time of the disease."[68]
What was dark was life; brightness belonged to death. Death
was stable, visible, legible, the *apriori* norm of modern
medical experience.

In the end, the living could be treated as dead because
every live body was going to die. "It is not because he
falls ill that man dies; fundamentally, it is because he
may die that man may fall ill."[69] One could not perform
autopsies on the living but through the use of instruments
the inner truth could be extracted and pulled into light.
Thus, intervention in a sick but alive body through machinery
amounted to a projective pathological anatomy. Moreover, the
use of instruments was endowed with a high moral tone. They
were cleaner. Revulsion and embarassment at the practice of
ausculation with plump women inspired the invention of the

stethoscope. Technology and moralism, the armature of power-
knowledge, was nearly complete. "The *libido sciendi*,
strengthened by the prohibition that it had aroused and
discovered, circumvents it by making it more imperious; it
provides itself with scientific and social justifications,
inscribing it within necessity in order to pretend the more
easily to efface it from the ethical, and to build upon it
the structure that traverses it and maintains it."[70] The
final step, already implicit in the question "where does it
hurt?" involved the elimination of disease as an essence or
complex of meaning: there formed in its stead the concept of
pathological life, of pathological reactions, and of patho-
genic agents, all of which traversed the body seen in the
harsh straight light of death. Life had been removed, and
with it the complex textures of reality, the uneven curved
landscape of nature. A new relationship between knowledge
and curing had been put into place: "the patient has to be
enveloped in a collective, homogeneous space."[71] And the
discourse that expressed medical knowledge was, in principle,
complete: everything that appeared to the clinical gaze could
be expressed; that which was not on the scale of the gaze fell
outside the domain of possible knowledge.

  The Birth of the Clinic, whose significance has often
been underestimated, in fact helped establish the agenda for
Foucault's later work.[72] First, it underlined the importance
to be attributed to the formation of knowledge, of scientific
discursive practices. The centrality of death in the knowledge of clinical medicine meant the expulsion of life.
"Western man could constitute himself in his own eyes as an
object of science . . . only in the opening created by his
own elimination: from the experience of unreason was born
psychology, the very possibility of psychology; from the
integration of death into medical thought is born a medicine
that is given as a science of the individual. And generally
speaking, the experience of the individual in modern culture

is bound up with that of death."[73] The relationship of
scientific discourse to the elimination of the individual
was taken up directly in Foucault's next two major studies.
Secondly, however, medical practice was part of a specific
configuration of power and had its own important role in
the great and unfinished western dogmatomachy. The ideology
of religious power, the self-interpretation of the ancien régime,
was, to the modern mind, based upon the fear of nature.
Included in the fear of nature was the fear of death: it
is "natural" to be afraid to die, which was why religion
provided so many symbolic (that is, interpretative) immort-
alities. But with the industrial and technical domination
of nature (and with the medical domestication of death)
religious self-interpretation gave way to the ideology of
atheist, liberal power. The end of religious fear was not the
end of fear. Social, not natural forces were henceforth the
sources of dread. Indeed, the very act of mastering nature
created the new social forces. Medicine responded to the
need to domesticate them, to control, supervise, and moralize
the mobile, fractious, dangerous industrial order. Liberal
and medical ideology combined in their vision of social order
as preservation of the normal. Change, that is, institutional
change, was assimilated to the category of pathology, which
introduced the notion, beloved by liberals, that so long as
institutions appeared to allow an individual to change his
social situation the question of changing the social order
was removed. And where was it removed to? To pathology,
sickness, madness, deviance, and criminality. Medicine,
therefore was an integral part of the disciplined, normalized post-historical bourgeois social order. This is the
topic of Foucault's most recent work.

THE ORIGIN OF SOCIAL SCIENCE

6

Although it was published three years later, *L'Archéologie du savoir* was in many respects continuous with *Les Mots et les choses*.[74] The later book is a systematic statement of the method used in the earlier studies and arose out of a series of discussions during which Foucault was requested to explain more explicitly what he had been up to.[75] Together they are an impressive account of the internal self-destruction of that modern comedy called social science, and can be warmly recommended on those grounds alone. The methodological reflections sought to justify the prior work and to create a solid basis for his subsequent studies. The actual topics discussed continued an inventory of modes of power-knowledge.

As in the earlier work, the aim was to analyze discontinuities, to establish differences, to avoid the reductive trap of teleology and pre-existing horizons, to give voice to a radically disjunctive temporality that does not promise the return of any dawn. This purpose was formalized as a discussion of a change in "episteme." By this neologism Foucault meant the context "in which knowledge envisaged apart from all criteria having reference to its rational value or to its objective forms, grounds its positivity and thereby manifests a history that is not that of its growing perfection, but rather that of its conditions of possibility." What counts in the historicity of knowledge, "what makes it possible to articulate the history of thought within itself, is its internal conditions of possibility."[76] An episteme was, therefore, an articulation of epistemological space that enabled any particular discourse to make sense as a discourse. At the same time, however, it was not an independent trans-

cendental realm but manifested itself by way of particular
discourses--by what was not said equally with what was said.
By definition, therefore, "in any given culture and at any
given moment there is always only one episteme that defines
the conditions of possibility of all knowledge, whether
expressed in a theory or silently invested in a practice."[77]
Archeology described the episteme of an era, the ensembles
of discursive and non-discursive practices that followed
certain rules, that got transformed, had phase-shifts and
residua, but that constituted not a condition of validity
for judgements but a condition of reality for statements.

It is, of course, important to know which speaker was
a member of what social group, but the *condition* for any
particular statement to be made has never resided in the
existence of a group. One must distinguish therefore between
two forms or levels of investigation. The first studied
opinions to see who belonged to what side of an argument
or discussion, to see what interests were at stake, what
the point of the argument was, how the struggle for power
developed. The other took no account of the personalities
involved nor their history and consisted solely in defining
the conditions on the basis of which any particular debate
and action, any particular deployment of power-knowledge,
was able to occur. "The first analysis would be the province
of a doxology. Archeology can recognize and practice only
the second."[78] To return to the example of medicine, Foucault's archeological investigation first showed there had
been a change of consciousness in the perception of illness.
After the French Revolution, it had political implications:
people with poor levels of health were seen to be likely to
revolt; the new manufacturing activity needed healthy workers.
Moreover, medicine could gain a universal application only
through the desacralization of the body, which permitted
autopsies and the possibility of looking at the body as an
instrument of labour; health became more important than

salvation. In addition, clinical discourse was related to
political discourse: society was understood an organic whole
with a functional coherence. Since nothing was given in
nature, nothing could be mastered simply through a command
of classificatory knowledge: technical intervention was
necessary to bring the truth into the open. And lastly, we
saw that these kinds of discursive changes were of a piece
with political or institutionalized power. The state defined
who had the right to practice medical speech (doctors, not
philosophers or farmers); clinicians determined what the object
of medical discourse was (illness as a statistical function of
a population), what would constitute medicalized space (what a
hospital was, and what went on there), the relationship of
medicine to society (a healthy society, a society in need of
treatment). None of the transformations in the conditions
of existence of medical discourse were rejected or translated
by the concepts of medical discourse: they modified the rules
of formation of those concepts. Political practice did not
transform medical objects (for example, what morbidity was)
but it did transform the system that offered a possible
object to medical discourse (for example, a population that
could be surveyed and given a medical profile, and provided
with a pathological evolution whose history was based on
the accumulation of information over a series of cases).
Political practice did not transform the methods of analysis
but the system of their formation: registration of sick
people and causes of death, hospital admission procedures
and record-keeping, the relationship of patients to hospital
staff, and so on. This relationship of political to medical
discourse was both direct, since it was not mediated by any
consciousness of the subjects to whom it was applied (rules
of admission to hospitals were to be followed not questioned:
if you wanted to get in, there was only one way), but also
indirect, since the actual practitioners of medical discourse
could not be considered simply as expressing a social or

economic interest. Unless one undertook to establish the
conditions of formation of a discursive practice (such as
was expressed in clinical medicine) one was forced either
to accept it as given, to acquiesce in the claims of the
technicians, or else to intervene directly by imposing
external and opposed criteria--reducing the practice involved
to psychological, economic, sociological, etc., categories.
But in neither case would one understand.[79]

In *The Order of Things*, Foucault discussed the discontinuities between the natural history, theory of wealth, and
general grammar of the classical period and the new sciences
of biology, political economy, and philology that were born
in and with the modern era. Secondly, he related these new
sciences to "man" as an object of knowledge. To the question,
what were the conditions under which a science of man has been
conceived to be possible? the answer was: only when the
existing episteme, the classical order of representation,
was eclipsed, only when non-representable realities were
discovered, only when men stopped asking "what does this
appearance mean?" and wondered "what lies in the depth
behind this misleading show?" Similitude and resemblance,
analogy, sympathy and antipathy, inscribed in the universe
by a system of signs, was seen to be the source of error and
confusion, not knowledge. Henceforth, things were to be clear
and distinct, analyzed in terms of identity and difference,
of measurement and order. Analysis became, in principle, a
universal procedure. The conditions of possibility of
living things were to be sought in life itself, the conditions
of exchange and profit in the fundamental activities of
labour, and the possibility of discourse and grammar in
the historical depth of languages, in systems of inflections,
modifications of stems, radicals and word endings. "Philology,
biology, and political economy were established not in the
places formerly occupied by general grammar, natural history,
and the analysis of wealth, but in an area where those forms

of knowledge did not exist, in the space they left blank, in
the deep gaps that separated their broad theoretical seg-
ments and that were filled with the murmur of the ontological
continuum. The object of knowledge in the nineteenth century
is formed in the very place where the classical plenitude
of being has fallen silent."[80] The discontinuities involved,
then, concerned fundamental arrangements of knowledge that
ordered specific discourses in such a way that it was possible
for those discourses to express beings in a system of names.

That a second change in episteme occurred in the years
after the French Revolution can be discovered by noting
certain signs scattered through the space of knowledge. New
positive sciences, the appearance of literature, which "said"
only itself and re-presented nothing, the reflection of philosophy on its own historical unfolding, in short, the emergence of history as both knowledge and the mode in which the
empirical order of things made their appearance. History
replaced the allegedly eternal classificatory grid of the
classical period where order had been the metaphor of truth.

In economics after Adam Smith, time was no longer a cycle
of impoverishment and wealth, nor of a linear increase attained
by astute policies that injected just the right amount of
circulating specie so that production increased more rapidly
than prices. Henceforth, time "was to be the interior time
of an organic structure that grows in accordance with its own
necessity and develops in accordance with autochthonous laws--
the time of capital and production."[81] Similarly in natural
history, one sought out functions, for these were the real
basis of classification. Characteristics were no longer
simply visible, nor established in the places formerly
occupied by general grammar, inscribed on the surface like
stripes on a tiger. "It is not because a character occurs
frequently in the structures observed that it is important;
it is because it is functionally important that it is often
encountered."[82] Classification meant relating what was

visible to what was more real, to its invisible and deeper
cause; only then would one rise from that hidden internal
architecture of organs to the surface display of bodily
signs. But the inside was not simply a secret text of the
outside, "it is the coherent totality of an organic structure
that weaves back into the unique fabric of its sovereignty
both the visible and the invisible."[83] Similarly again in
the study of languages, not sound, not sheer surface audi-
bility, but a skeletal "mechanism" determined individuality
and resemblance among languages. That is, there existed
within language an inflectional system, a hidden internal
architecture that governed the way that words were modified
in accordance with the explicit and visible grammatical
position they took up with one another.

To summarize Foucault's argument: the interpretation
of resemblance, representation, proportion, analogy and so
on gave way in the classical period to creations of order,
that is, to a grid of signs, a system of logical operations.
The theory of money and value was a "science of the signs
that authorize exchange and permit the establishment of
equivalences between men's needs or desires;" natural
history was "the science of the characters that articulate
the continuity and tangle of nature;" general grammar was
"the science of the signs by means of which men group together their individual perceptions and pattern the continuous
flow of their thoughts."[84] But when these old sciences
dissolved, when the project of an exhaustive ordering of
the world was abandoned, when men no longer sought knowledge
in the form of tabular categories, several important sequences
followed. The most general was that labour, life, and
language appeared as "transcendentals" that made possible
knowledge of living beings, of the laws of production, of
the forms of language. "In their being they are outside
knowledge, but by that very fact they are conditions of
knowledge."[85] That is, there was a displacement of being

with regard to appearance for which Kant provided the first
philosophical statement.[86]   In consequence, there arose a
metaphysics of the object "or, more exactly, metaphysics of
that never objectionable depth from which objects rise up
towards our superficial knowledge" and, in contrast, there
also arose the specialized sciences whose task was exhausted
in observation of what could be known positively.[87]   From
this division between formal, *apriori*, mathematical sciences
based on logic, and non-formal, *aposteriori,* empirical
sciences that employ logic in a fragmentary and localized
way, from this new dialectic of mathematical rigor and
erudition, there grew, naturally enough, a concern for a
unifying synthesis. Those who wished to see everything
hard-wired established a hierarchy of knowledge on the basis
of mathematics, developed elaborate reflections on the empirical methods of induction in the hopes of providing their
science with a philosophical foundation and formal, quasi-
mathematical justification, and advocated programmes for
the eventual transcription of economics, biology, linguistics
(and all the other social sciences) into mathematical formulae.
Their opponents affirmed an impossibility: life is too
specific; the social sciences do not lend themselves to
methodological reduction. All that is gained by the attempt
is distortion and ignorance of it. This debate, which began
at the start of the modern era, continues on its tedious,
repetitive way even today. But besides this general consequence specific changes were also introduced.

Classical discussion of economic factors consisted in
constructing a tabular space where all values were able to
represent each other. Prices increased, for example, when
the representing elements, namely money, went up faster
than the elements represented, namely things. But, with
Ricardo, labour was displaced with respect to representation; it resided in a realm of its own, where representation had no power. Labour was organized according to its

own causality. It could accumulate on its own. It could be
embodied. Accordingly, it broke the table of reciprocal
determinations. Henceforth there could exist an organization
of wealth in a temporal sequence, in history. There was, for
example a change in the meaning of scarcity. No longer was
it a function of need in men's minds, that is, of representation (bread is scarce for the poor, diamonds for the
rich), but constituted a fundamental insufficiency independent
of men's opinions. That is, "it is no longer in the interplay
of representation that economics finds its principle, but near
that perilous region where life is in confrontation with
death."[88] Labour, then, was the means of temporarily avoiding
death. Economic man did not represent his needs to himself
and the objects capable of satisfying them: "he is the human
being who spends, wears out, and wastes his life in evading
the imminence of death. He is a finite being."[89] The previous
discussion of needs by economists was then taken over by
psychologists.

Human finitude infected the ground metaphor of history
as well. For Ricardo the end of history was a decline in
the rate of profit which eventually led to a steady state.
Labour, production, accumulation, and growth of real costs
constituted history; the motor of the process was the
finitude of man and the succession of generations, but also
the embodied bequests of their labours. "The more man makes
himself at home in the heart of the world, the farther he
advances his possession of nature, the more strongly also
does he feel the pressure of his finitude, and the closer
he comes to his own death."[90] The options of the end of
history were narrow. In fact, there were two.

The first saw a gradual and deliberate but slow movement towards stability whose weight of existence alone justified history as its goal, as what history never had ceased
to be from the start. This was Ricardo's option: a self-
limitation of scarcity through demographic stabilization.

"Life and death will fit exactly one against the other, surface
to surface; . . . subjected to the great erosion of History,
man will gradually be stripped of everything that might hide
him from his own eyes; he will have exhausted all the possible
elements that tend to blur and disguise beneath the promises
of time his anthropological nakedness; by long but inevitable
and tyrannical paths, History will have led man to the truth
that brings him to a halt face to face with himself."[91] With
Ricardo, then, one can see a grandfather of bureaucratic order,
of tough-minded demographers lecturing backward and prolific
peoples on the necessities of family planning and the virtues
of norm and regularity. Beside them, one cannot help but
notice the smiling face of benevolent trilateral men and the
foundations that fund the demographic wisdom. The foulness
of the sight helps sustain the present zeal of those who
choose the other option.

This was the option of Marx. History was indeed moving,
but it was moving towards a point of reversal where it was
fixed only insofar as it suppressed what it had never ceased
to be from the start. History, that is, engendered revolution and the beginning of a time that had neither the same
form, nor the same laws, nor the same mode of passing. The
Revolution was to bring forth a new and final man, whom Marx
called socialist man. But both Marx and Ricardo, Foucault
said, were two sides of the same epistemic coin. There was
no difficulty in understanding who chose Ricardo and who
chose Marx, nor why they did so. "But these are merely
derived differences which stem first and last from a doxol-
ogical investigation and treatment."[92] In other words, the
conflict between Marxist economics and bourgeois economics
was a family spat. "Their controversies may have stirred
up a few waves and caused a few surface ripples; but they
are no more than storms in a children's paddling pool."[93]
Both, that is, were essentially transcendental speculations
that moved within the restrictive horizon of the end of

history.

It made little difference how the accent of anthropological finitude was placed, whether the dénouement was a slow
erosion or a violent eruption, a whimper or a bang. Either
way the post-historical truth would emerge in stony immobility.
The calendar would still run up numbers because the planet
revolved, but the years would be no more than numbers, a void.
"The flow of development, with all its resources of drama,
oblivion, alienation, will be held within an anthropological
finitude that finds in them, in turn, its own illuminated
expression. Finitude, with its truth, is posited in time;
and time is therefore finite. The great dream of an end to
History is the utopia of causal systems of thought, just as
the dream of the world's beginnings was the utopia of the
classifying systems of thought."[94] In Nietzsche one may find
this theme aglow for the last time. Indeed, he destroyed
it by transforming the end of history into the death of God
and the double odyssey of the last man. Finitude was still
the basis of the superman, but the chain of history that Hegel
wished to dominate with his magic words had been bent around,
like a snake swallowing its tail, as the eternal return.
It was Nietzsche, that is, "who burned for us, even before
we were born, the intermingled promises of the dialectic
and anthropology."[95] We find ourselves with the results of
Nietzsche's incineration, reading by a light that may be
either the revived flame of his final combustion, the flash-
ing and threatening presence of unreason, or the light of
dawn.

The development of biology led to an exactly opposite
consequence. Under the pressure of intervention through
dissection and anatomy, the great classifications of the
great classical age gave way to functional systems. By
cutting up bodies, dividing them into distinct portions,
fragmenting them in space, one could see resemblances that
remained invisible externally. Classical natural history

gave precedence to plants because an endless table of their
external differences best expressed the essence of living
being. Modern biology is centered on animals, however, for
they best manifest the enigmas of life. "Transferring its
most secret essence from the vegetable to the animal kingdom,
life has left the tabulated space of order and become wild
once more. The same movement that dooms it to death reveals
it as murderous. It kills because it lives. Nature can no
longer be good . . . life can no longer be separated from
murder, nature from evil, or desires from anti-nature."[96]
Life and death were again joined: death was spent life,
mere being was the non-being of life. Thus it happened
that beings were inconsequential and transitory figures,
temporary porters of life who presumed to maintain its
presence by their mere will to survive. "And so, for biological knowledge, the being of things is an illusion, a veil
that must be torn aside in order to reveal the mute and
invisible violence that is devouring them in the darkness."[97]
Thus the contradiction of economics and biology: the one
embraced the end of history, the other proclaimed the
infinity of life; the one recognized the real production
of things by labour, the other dissipated all claims in
the distant rumble of death; the one, embossed with the
signature of necessity was also lightened by the promise
of great rewards in time, the other, marked by living
continuities that created beings only in order to dissolve
them again, was for that reason freed from all historical
limitations.

      And thirdly, there were specific consequences for
language. No longer conceived as a system of artificial
symbols and logical operations, no longer linked to the
knowing of unequivocal things, language gained an historical
depth. It was defined by its own internal laws of grammar,
and expressed the freedom of human destiny. There were no
formal rules and categories but only the spoken life of a

people. Nineteenth-century philology was full of profound
political implications. First of all it was nationalist, but
then it grew cosmopolitan. "All languages have an equal
value: they simply have different internal structures.
Hence that curiosity for rare, little spoken, poorly 'civil-
ized' languages, of which Rask gave an example with his
great voyage of enquiry through Scandanavia, Russia, the
Caucasus, Persia, and India."[98] Looked at through the lens
of philology, the first volume of *Capital* was an exegesis of
the term "value;" Nietzsche wrote the exegesis of a few words
of ancient Greek, and Freud provided the exegesis "of all
those unspoken phrases that support and at the same time under-
mine our apparent discourse, our fantasies, our dreams, our
bodies." In its contemporary form, philology became criticism.
It sought "to destroy syntax, to shatter tyrannical modes of
speech, to turn words around in order to perceive all that is
being said through them and despite them."[99] In contrast and
in contradiction to philology and criticism was literature.
Literature had no purpose other than to affirm its own perceptions of existence; it was utterly detached from the grid
of virtues that marked the classical period: taste, natural-
ism, truth, piety, moderation, and so on. Now it has become,
as Foucault showed in his study of Roussel, "a silent, cautious
deposition of the word upon the whiteness of a piece of paper,
where it can possess neither sound nor interlocutor, where
it has nothing to say but itself, nothing to do but shine
in the brightness of its being."[100] The opposition of
biology and economics was reduplicated within language.
It has become internally fragmented and we are left alone
with the fragile vibrations of words. But even diremptions
have a context; even contradictions occur within a field
that encompasses the contending poles. For modern thought,
it was the ambiguous object of knowledge, of the specialized sciences, who was also the subject who knows, who
created those sciences, namely man, the observed spectator.

The profound and fundamental intention of knowledge in
the classical period was to create a table or picture of
reality or even a picture-reality. Classical language was
a discourse common to representation and things; it did not
distinguish what was represented from the appearance of
representation. In contrast, modern discourse considered
representation not as the identity of a thing but only in
its relation to the human being, to man. The contents of
man's knowledge revealed to him what he knew was external,
other than himself; it passed through him as though he were
a natural object, "a face doomed to be erased in the course
of history." Because man knew, he knew he was finite; no
eternity, no infinity, no "after-life."[101] As long as the
empirical contents of knowledge were situated within the
space of representation, a metaphysics of the infinite was
necessary so that, on the one hand, the empiricities remained
finite and yet, as representations, found the locus of their
truth within an infinite and eternal order. "But when these
empirical contents were detached from representation and
contained the principle of their existence within themselves,
then a metaphysics of infinity became useless: from that
point on, finitude never ceased to refer back to itself."[102]
Awareness of finitude, of the limitedness of knowledge, spelled
the end to metaphysics: "the philosophy of life denounces
metaphysics as a veil of illusion, that of labour denounces
it as an alienated form of thought and an ideology, that of
language as a cultural episode."[103] So, the end of metaphysics was coeval with modernity, with the advent of man,
of anthropology, and of humanism.

At the level of appearance, modernity began when the
human being first existed only within his physiology, the
organism, the armature of his limbs, the shell of his head;
when he first existed at the centre of a labour by whose
laws he was governed but whose product escaped him; when
he first thought in a language so much older than himself

that he could not know all that he said. But beneath those
appearances was the fundamental reality of finitude.
"Modern culture can conceive of man because it conceives
of the truth on the basis of itself."[104] Man, then, was
a product of the finite thought that began in the eighteenth
century. Before then, culture was concerned with God, with
the cosmos, with resemblances of things, with the laws of
space and time, and also with the body and the passions and
the imagination, but not with man, not with an object of
knowledge that could be the subject of an historical development, finite but endless.

To call modernity into question, to pierce the horizon
of the end of history and survey the contours of post-
historical life one must ask: does man exist? "To imagine,
for an instant, what the world and thought and truth might
be if man did not exist, is considered to be merely indulging
in paradox. This is because we are so blinded by the recent
manifestation of man that we can no longer remember a time--
it is not so long ago--when the world, its order, and human
beings existed, but man did not."[105] Man was a creature of
the modern episteme. To understand what modernity meant one
must stand outside that episteme, one must already be post-
modern, which is precisely Foucault's claim. Only if
modernity could be seen for what it was, a limited episode,
an era bounded by the classical period and contemporary
post-history, could its consequences be seen and properly
understood. It goes without saying that one cannot understand the historical or modern era from within pre-modern
classical categories: the calendar unfolds only in one
direction. There can be no return along that historical
timeline to pre-history. Thus, while one can sympathize
with the motivations of those who hanker nostalgically for
the classical, eternal categories of the true and the
beautiful and the good, who conceive of the great dogmatomachy as between the "ancients" and the "moderns," and,

revolted by modernity, resolutely choose the side of the
ancients, one can do no more than sympathize. Simply to
conceive the question that way is an historical and modern
exercise. To think beyond modernity one must think beyond
history, not before it.

Two sets of consequences are important for the theme
of power-knowledge. First, man had no identity. Because
man was finite, he was both himself and other. He is
what he is now and also what preceded him since what came
before constituted the depth of his historicity, and was
what gave momentum to his present activities. Accordingly,
he had no identity because what was his origin, what was
original in man, was always bound to be other than what
he is. "It is that which introduces into his experience
contents and forms older than him, which he cannot master;
its often mutually irreducible chronologies scatter him
through time and pinion him at the centre of the duration
of things."[106] So far as the social sciences were concerned, the three domains of biology, economics, and the
study of language provided three heterogeneous and irreducible models. If the biological model was adopted, man
appeared as a being possessing physical, chemical, cultural,
etc., stimuli, who would react, adapt, evolve, submit, in
such a way that one could observe "norms of adjustment that
permit him to perform his functions." If the model was
economic, man appeared as a being having needs and desires.
He sought to satisfy them, and so had interests, searched
after profits, was in opposition to others, and was therefore in a situation of irreducible conflict that nevertheless was governed by rules. If the model was language,
man appeared as an attempt to say something. Every gesture
had a meaning, even failures and involuntary actions. He
arranged objects, rites, rituals, customs, ceremonies, and
discourses around him in such a way that they constituted
a system of signs. "Thus, these three pairs, of function

and norm, conflict and rule, signification and system, completely cover the entire domain of what can be known about man."[107] All of these pairs can drift between the various domains even though they belonged primarily to one or another. In this way all the sciences of man interlocked which was why it was always difficult to separate strictly literary criticism from economic history, sociology from psychology, and so on. Moreover, these pairs had an internal history. Generally one can plot a succession from biology (man is analyzed "romantically" as an organic whole in terms of specific psychic, group, social and cultural-linguistic functions), to economics (man is the locus of conflicts in the process of resolution), to philology (man must be interpreted and his hidden meanings uncovered), or linguistics (man is a signifying system whose structure must be clarified.) Thus we move from Comte, to Marx, to Freud and Saussure.

    A second consequence: modern thought has never been able to propose a morality, an ethics, or a political theory. This was not because it was too speculative but, just the opposite, because it was a mode of action. "For modern thought, no morality is possible. Thought had already 'left' itself in its own being as early as the nineteenth century; it is no longer theoretical. As soon as it functions it offends or reconciles, attracts or repels, breaks, dissociates, unites or reunites; it cannot help but liberate or enslave."[108] This aspect of modern thought was understood even by the profoundly stupid who declared all thought to be either "progressive" or "reactionary," or that no philosophy could be independent of political choice.[109] Their stupidity, or perhaps merely their laziness, lay in the belief that all thought must "express" the ideology of a class: Socrates turned into an "elitist" and an apologist for the rich because he hung around with aristocratic young men. (One of Nietzsche's

funniest jokes made Socrates "express" the ideology of the
ugly. Why not?) Their completely involuntary profundity
lay in the fact that such views focus directly upon the
specifically modern mode of being of thought. Knowledge
of man, unlike the sciences of nature, always involved
political action. Again, as concerns the sciences of man,
one can see easily the unhappy consequences. Here the
first term of each of the constituent pairs (that is,
function, conflict, and signification) receded and the
second term (norm, rule, and system) gained in intensity
and importance. So long as the functional point of view
was more important than the normative, then non-normal
functions were as acceptable as normal ones; pathological
psychology was as legitimate as normal psychology, pathological or irrational societies or quasi-morbid beliefs were
as acceptable as normal ones. So long as conflict was more
important than rule, it was assumed that some kinds of
conflicts were inevitable, that individual existence and
the existence of societies involved risk and that a regime
of perpetual peace was confined to the tomb. So long as
signification carried more weight than system, a division
between the significant and the non-significant could be
made: meaning existed in some areas of human activity but
not in others and no one tried to imagine that everything
had to have a meaning. However, when analysis was confined
to norm, rule, and system, each of these terms provided its
own coherence and validity. Everything may be thought
within those terms, and nothing legitimate, acceptable,
or meaningful resided outside.

The appearance of man, then, "was not the liberation
of an old anxiety, the transition into luminous consciousness
of an age-old concern, the entry into objectivity of something
that had long remained trapped within beliefs and philoso-
phies: it was the effect of a change in the fundamental
arrangements of knowledge. As the archeology of our thought

easily shows, man is an invention of recent date. And one
perhaps nearing its end." A similar reorganization of
knowledge to that which caused classical thought to crumble
would erase man "like a face drawn in sand at the edge of
the sea."[110] This is why, for Foucault, Nietzsche was so
important and so disturbing. For he was the first to tell
that man would be no more, that there would be supermen and
submen. Within the philosophy of the return, this meant
that man had long since disappeared and was continuing to
do so. This was why, for Foucault, Nietzsche "marks the
threshold beyond which contemporary philosophy can begin
thinking again; and he [i.e., Nietzsche] will no doubt
continue for a long while to dominate its advance. If the
discovery of the Return is indeed the end of philosophy,
then the end of man, for its part, is the return of the
beginning of philosophy. It is no longer possible to think
in our day other than in the void of man's disappearance.
For this void does not create a deficiency; it does not
constitute a lacuna that must be filled. It is nothing
more, and nothing less, than the unfolding of a space in
which it is once more possible to think."[111] There was,
then, an uncompatibility between "man" and the sciences
of man, between the signs and their meaning. The science
of man was a fraud or an idol and, in any event, the
humanist era has finally been closed, not by a man named
Michel Foucault who wrote a few books about it, but because
the sciences that were supposed to liberate man have in
fact led to his dissolution.

    With *Les Mots et les choses* and *L'archéologie du savoir*
the brush has been cleared and the stumps have been pulled.
Now, in this clearing, one can sow new seeds, make new
plantings, raise new crops, but *not* reap the harvest of a
final knowledge. Within the philosophy of the return,
knowledge is always back-to-back with non-knowledge and
can be understood only by way of it. There is a fearful

openness in this: we have no destiny but are charged with
creating our own.[112]   Who, then, is my enemy and who my
friend? "We all struggle against each other. And there
is something in each of us that struggles against something else in us."[113]   That struggle is without an end;
it is forever decentring itself and is given over to making
differences, not imposing regularities under the pretence
of discovering truth. That great game is finished.

DISCURSIVE PRACTICE AND POWER

7

   The Archeology of Knowledge was, as has been said, a
methodological postscript to *The Order of Things*. In the
second work he tried to clear up certain misunderstandings
that had arisen in the wake of the popular success of *The
Order of Things*. These had to do with his relationship
to "structuralism" as an intellectual movement, with the
question of the disappearance of "man," and with periodi-
zation in history. Foucault was led to examine terms such
as tradition, influence, development, and so on, as well as
grand categories such as science, literature, politics,
fiction, etc. The two most interesting of the grand
categories, and the most slippery, were book and *oeuvre*.
Here he was concerned to determine what he called the discursive unity of a book, of which the physical volume is
the material support, and the expressive function of the
collection of tomes that constitute an *oeuvre*. The book,
the *oeuvre,* the collection that forms a discipline, these
things, said Foucault, were made up of statements that had
the character of historical events as their most significant feature. Statements were associated into what he
termed discursive formations--such as clinical medicine
and psychiatry.
   Foucault made an elaborate analysis of the difference
between a statement and a proposition or a sentence. Statements were historical: they were not once and for all
meanings, but appeared in a specific context, with a
specific status; it could enter into "various networks
and various fields of use, be subjected to transferences
or modifications, be integrated into operations and

strategies in which its identity is maintained or effaced.
Thus the statement circulates, is used, disappears, allows
or prevents the realization of desire, serves or resists
various interests, participates in challenge and struggle,
and becomes a theme of appropriation and rivalry."[114]
Statements, and collections of them in discourse being neither
eternal nor inexhaustible treasures of meaning, were limited,
finite, and useful. And for that reason they were the
objects of desire and will and power. Statements, Foucault
said, were "assets" and so inherently the object of
political struggle.

There followed a further elaboration of what, with
some embarassment, Foucault called a "bizarre machinery."
This included terms such as positivity, the archive, the
historical *apriori* and the term archeology itself. Together they constituted a new "arsenal," that is, a
collection of weapons to be employed in future battles.
The military imagery was deliberate: Foucault understood
his archeology as inherently polemical.

For some scholars of the history of ideas, the notion
of a discursive *practice* was already an anethema. What is
worse, rather than remain in the pristine world of ideas,
Foucault insisted upon relating discursive practices with
one another and with non-discursive practices. But he did
so in a limited way, without claiming, for example, to
provide a complete picture of the classical world. Instead,
he was interested in showing the specific relations between,
say, biology and political economy, or natural history and
the analysis of wealth, but more importantly, he sought to
show how political practices took part in the formation
of discourse. For example, the conscript armies of the
Napoleonic period and the necessities of their organization
led to new forms of medical control based on norms and
enunciated by the doctor and only by him. Later, in peace
time, medical discourse and medical control could be extended

to the civil population under the banner of public health.
The political significance of the relationship of discursive to non-discursive practice was suggested with the
closing dialogue to *The Archeology of Knowledge.*

The intention of this dialogue was to anticipate
misunderstandings and try to characterize the argument of
the book, to show, for example how archeology was not
structuralism or how it was not quite history or philosophy
either. And he ended it, appropriately enough, by raising
additional questions. If one saw discourse as a thin
transparency, shining at the limit of things and thought,
what was its political status? Had not the twin practices
of revolutionary political and revolutionary scientific
discourse removed the notion that words were an external
whisper, difficult to hear in the loud importances of
history? "Or must we conclude that in order to refuse this
lesson, you are determined to misunderstand discursive
practices, in their own existence, and that you wished to
maintain, in spite of that lesson, a history of mind, of
rational knowledge, ideas and opinions?" Such stubbornness
and apparent failure of the imagination was in fact a failure
of nerve: why reply in terms of consciousness when the
question deals with practice? "What is that fear that makes
you seek, beyond all boundaries, raptures, shifts and divisions,
the great historico-transcendental destiny of the Occident?"
Whatever the fear may be, it was clear to Foucault that it
would not be dispelled by more words. On the contrary:
"It **seems** to me that the only reply to this question is a
political one. But let us leave that to one side for today.
Perhaps we will take it up soon in another way."[115] It was
a curious sort of politics that he had in mind, since he
concluded his book with a gesture of sympathy to those who
saw in his own discursive practice, his archeology, a threat
to the immortality they had hoped to gain through words.
For Foucault, however, words said only themselves, and no

one could speak on behalf of anyone else.

Between the enigmatic politics that closed *The Arch-eology* and the enigmatic events of May, 1968, their exists an interrelationship. Raymond Aron called it a *révolution introuvable*; he was right though not perhaps for the reasons he set forth in his hostile account. It had no centre because the state had no centre; De Gaulle was not a symbol of a fantastic regal order but a source of laughter; spokes-men and leaders were required by the media and they appeared, but in order to mock and outrage.[116] One of the results of May was the creation of an academic asylum in the Vincennes Park. There the leftists could do what they wished and stay out of harm's way. Foucault was appointed head of the philosophy department. In this role he deliv-ered a series of lectures on Nietzsche, whom he later described as the philosopher of power just as Marx was the philosopher of relations of production.[117] He would, he said, *use* Nietzsche's thought; the only valid tribute to thought such as Nietzsche's, he said, was "to make it groan and protest."[118] Nietzsche, then, was Foucault's tool-box. The most important instrument he withdrew from it was the concept of will-to-knowledge, a term closely associated with will-to-power. The subject of knowledge, he said, was not neutral or passionless or committed solely to truth but bursting with instinctive passions, with the devotion of an inquisitor, a cruel subtlety and malice. The will-to-knowledge violated those who were happy in their ignorance and delighted in discoveries that disturb the universe. The will-to-knowledge was rancorous; it rested upon injustice and maliciousness, and knew neither limit nor moderation.[119] In 1970 Foucault entered the Collège de France, and in his inaugural lecture deployed his newly re-tooled Nietzschean arms.

The Order of Discourse[120] was a magnificent example of Foucault's irony and wit in action. Topically, it was

a discussion of discussion or rather, of the constraints
that mutilate discussion; it was an innaugural lecture
whose first words expressed the desire not to begin.
But, he had to begin; besides there was the institution,
the Collège de France, that solemnized beginnings and
imposed ritual forms and established orders. Foucault
was called to speak in a place that "honours and disarms"
discourse so that whatever power it had would be owed to
the institution, not the speaker. "I am assuming," he
said, "that in every society the production of discourse
is at once controlled, selected, organized and redistri-
buted according to a certain number of procedures whose
role is to avert its powers and its dangers, to master
chance events, and to evade their ponderous, awesome
materiality."[121] The first procedure excluded. It
operated by prohibition, by division or categorization
and rejection, or by the opposition of true and false.

Prohibition appeared as taboo: "we know perfectly
well we are not free to say just anything." It was also
constrained by circumstance and by role: "not just
anyone can speak of just anything." On the contrary,
certified speakers delivered discourses on approved topics
at auspicious occasions--such as the present event that
Foucault was so gaily subverting. Prohibition through
categorization was preeminent in the way the discourses of
madmen had been understood, namely as utterly unreasonable
or as harbouring a deep but hidden wisdom. On its own
the discourse of the mad did not exist. The exclusions
of truth, at first sight, seemed hardly to be exclusions
at all since they did not seem to be arbitrary or historically conditioned. And yet, Foucault said, if we ask
not whether knowledge is false or true but *why* one wishes
to know, the exclusions of will appear clearly enough.
Changes in the understanding of truth, from the classical
to the modern period, for example, were based on a system

of exclusion. Moreover it was perfectly geared to non-
discursive practices, to actual institutions that undertook the selection, organization and distribution of
discourses in society. But if truth was never seen as
constraint, that was only because its informing will was
always masked. And rarely, as with Nietzsche, Artaud,
Roussel, or Bataille, when the will to truth turned against
truth and tried to tear off its mask, which generally meant
to violate taboos, expectations and roles, or to object to
the external definitions of madness, the result stood as
a signpost pointing the way that Foucault's own work would
follow.

A second set of procedures operated within discourse
itself so as to regulate its unpredictability. Commentary
re-stated what had already been said and by that activity
refined and controlled it; the concept of an author imposed
a unifying principle and a biographic consistency, a
tameness to discourse; and disciplines enabled us to
construct, within a narrow framework a quasi-anonymous
body of propositions, rules, definitions and techniques
for the production of truth.

A third group of rules was concerned neither with
mastering the powers of discourse nor with controlling the
unpredictabilities of appearance but with determining the
conditions under which discourses were spoken, and who would
be allowed to speak them. There were ritual qualifications
that speakers must meet; there were societies devoted to
specialized speech; there were doctrinal clubs and associ-
ations where the truth circulated like a breeze; finally,
there was the social appropriation of discourse into
educational systems that served the political function
of socialization, which is to say, to transmit knowledge
and power to a few. With all these procedures in operation,
a law or system of discourse has been produced governed by
an internally defined rationality that is the principle of

its expression and that therefore denies the particular and restrictive reality of itself as a discourse. On its own understanding it must simply be truth. But it was not: it was a practice and perhaps a violence done to things, some of which were human and some of which were not.

As Alan Sheridan rightly observed, in *The Order of Discourse,* as in his previous books, power was conceived as a limitation and a constraint. Foucault had not yet discovered that power was productive, that it produced discourse and thereby produced truth.[122]

PIERRE RIVIÈRE

8

After 1970, much of Foucault's work was initially undertaken as preparation for lectures at the Collège de France or
for his seminar. The results have been published in essays
by several hands as well as in monographs and in the *Annuaire*.
The range of subject-matter was enormous; the lens by which
it was all focussed remained power-knowledge. Some of the
terminology changed. Foucault spoke less of archeology or
of a change in episteme and more of discursive practices,
which, he said, were "characterized by the partitioning of
a field of objects, by the definition of a legitimate perspective for the subject of knowledge, and by fixing norms
for the elaboration of concepts and theories. Each of them
therefore assumes a system of prescriptions that govern
exclusions and choices."[123] Conflicts in discursive
practices could take place within the same episteme as well
as between two epistemes during a period of transition or
consolidation. Later he introduced the term *dispositif*,
device, apparatus, disposition of devices etc. An episteme,
he said, was a discursive *dispositif*, and therefore a more
limited concept. A *dispositif* had three characteristics or
aspects. First, it involved a heterogeneous collection of
discourses, institutions, architectural arrangements, rules,
laws, administrative decrees, scientific discussions, philosophical and ethical propositions, philanthropic notions,
and so on. The *dispositif* was the conceptual and practical
line along which these apparently unconnected things could
all be unified. Second, it involved the mode of relations
among all these elements, how discourses changed meaning,
how they were related to institutions, and so on. Third,

it involved a formative act that, at any given moment, responded to an emergency and so had a dominant strategic function. For example, industrialization implied a strategic imperative to deal with an unstable and floating population of vagabonds, madmen, bandits, etc., that, little by little, resulted in the *dispositif* that controlled madness, mental illness, delinquents, etc. Not all of the consequences were intended; there was no implication that the strategy was complete or perfect. Yet, once an institution was in place the results of its activity could be bent to conform more or less with the original imperative.[124]

The first of these collective efforts, and one that showed in a most spectacular way the conflict of discourses within the *dispositif* of power-knowledge was entitled *Moi, Pierre Rivière, ayant égorgé ma mère, ma soeur, et mon frère . . . .*[125] The title was taken from the opening lines of Rivière's confession, which was itself entitled "Details and explanation of the event that took place on June 3rd at Aunay, a village in Fauctrie, written by the author of this action." The facts were clear and distinct and were stated in the title of Foucault's book. Pierre Rivière, a Norman peasant, 20 years old, slaughtered his mother, his sister, and his brother. The confession and other discourses reproduced in this book or hovering in the wings, were all concerned with what the event meant. The medico-juridical issue was also clear: did the events and the confession mean that Rivière was sane and should be executed, or that he was crazy and should be hospitalized?

According to Rivière's own account, he was a normal enough child until, when he was about ten or twelve, he decided not to become a priest. Then he started to act rather odd. According to the lawyers, he was always sane; according to one set of doctors, he was always mad. Both contradicted Rivière who said there was a decisive change

when he was ten or twelve. Thus, "the elaboration of the
picture of Rivière, in each of these two accounts, does
not work towards reconstituting his story; it defines a
grid that operates to select from the facts reported by
Rivière and by those who testified; it institutes an
encoding that allows the facts to be interpreted."[126]
The magistrates selected facts that showed permanent
features of Rivière's character: he was intelligent,
opinionated, and cruel. The first doctor who examined
him, Bouchard, did not disagree. Using traditional
commonsense and the old theory of humors, he said Rivière
was sane. He had suffered no blows to head, no organic
problems, so Bouchard could see nothing medical in the
case at all.

Not so the others. Vastel, the second doctor, was a
provincial notable, a specialist from Caen, and was retained
by the defence. (Bouchard had been retained by the pros-
ecution; the presumption of the lawyers was that, if you
wanted to save a defendant's neck, get the specialists on
your side.) Vastel's vocabulary was technical but arbitrary and imprecise. In any case, it was clear to him that
Rivière was mad, and had always been mad. For example,
Rivière said that, as a child, one of his games was to
torture frogs and birds. It gave him pleasure, he said,
though it was obviously cruel. No, said Vastel, it was
evidence of religious mania since he was reproducing the
scenes of Christ's passion. Why? because he was a
religious maniac. Vastel was, in effect, a semi-specialist,
allied to the new science of psychiatry but hardly at the
centre of its power-knowledge. That was in Paris. The
Parisians—Esquirol, Orfila, Marc, Pariset, Rostan, Mitivié,
and Leuret—stuck to documents and never examined the
defendant. The most important factor in their intervention
was their signatures, the greatness of their names, and the
importance of their positions. The purpose of their peti-

tion (after a desire to see justice done, of course) was to
ensure that the social application of their science was
properly defended, and the finding of the jury, that the
clearly insane Pierre Rivière was guilty, was a defeat for
the entire body of specialists.   "Seven medical luminaries
would not bestir themselves in 1835 on behalf of some
murderer they had never seen.   They were making a demon-
stration of their power."[127]   They certainly did not give
any advice or therapy.   In other words, all that was
involved was a conflict in the form of social control.
Behind the apparatus of penal justice loomed the shadow
of the guillotine and the imperative: "guilty: off with
his head!"   Behind the apparatus of psychiatric medicine
was the shadow of the asylum and its imperative: "too sick
for society; away he must go!"   In the event, Rivière went
to the Beaulieu asylum, *à perpétuité*; five years was all he
could take, then he hanged himself in his cell.

      Whatever else may be said of Rivière, he was certainly
excessive.   When working with his father he would load too
many stones on the wagon; his children's game, when he pre-
tended cabbages were humans whose heads he would chop up,
destroyed too much food; too many frogs and birds were
crucified; his laughter was too uncontrolled and especially
his crime was too much: he did not just kill somebody, he
killed three members of his own family, including his
pregnant mother,[128] and he didn't just kill them, he hacked
them into a pulpy mess.   Why? This was what Rivière said:
"I wholly forgot the principles which should have made me
respect my mother and my sister and my brother, I regarded
my father as being in the power of mad dogs or savages
against whom I must take up arms, religion prohibited such
things, but I paid no attention to its rules, it even seemed
to me that God had destined me for this and I would be
executing his justice.   I knew the rules of men, but I
thought myself wiser than them.   I regarded them as base

and shameful."[129] He wished to deliver his father whom he
loved from the tyranny of a domineering wife; his siblings
took their mother's side, so they had to be killed too. He
knew that what he had done was, in the language of the penal
code, un-natural. The only thing worse was cannibalism.[130]
Thus, he fled into nature. "At last I resolved to conform
to my state, seeing that the evil was irreparable; I
resolved to live on herbs and roots until events took their
course." If he survived, it would be as an animal. But he
lacked the instincts of an animal as much as he lacked the
culture of a human. He was without enunciation, without
any intelligible appearance or persona by which others could
recognize him. His return to society took the form of a
minimal enunciation: he conceived of the notion, while in
the bush, of returning as a madman.

At the close of his memoir, Rivière said he looked
forward to his execution, which "must put an end to all my
resentment." His act and his writing were two parts of the
same gesture. Originally he had planned to write his account
of what he was going to do, do it, mail the account to the
authorities, and finally be himself killed. Then he revised
his plan: he would write about his parents' troubles and
then, later, in a second text explain why he had to kill
his mother, and lastly, he would do it. And then there was
the final plan: kill, give himself up, write about it, die.
Save for the 29 days of flight, it conformed to the actual
course of events. In other words, he knew that by killing
his mother, he was sacrificing himself for the sake of his
father.[131] That particular bit of discursive practice
seemed not to have gained any visibility at his trial.
Indeed, it was assumed by the lawyers and the doctors that
the words of a peasant could not possibly hold any integral
meaning: peasants were, by definition, mute. Their only
acts were their deeds, which the savants, with competence
and confidence, alone were capable of interpreting. For

Rivière, however, his memoir was to bring him visibility.
That was why, as Vastel said, after answering the examining doctors query, he would return immediately to his
writing as if the investigation were an interruption,
which it was. That was why, as well, Rivière compared
himself with Napoleon: Napoleon had many people killed
only for his own glory. By comparison Pierre was not so
bad: he killed but three people (four including himself)
in order to free his father. And yet, in this battle of
power-knowledge the odds were greatly against him. His
memoir was neglected. It was not suppressed, but it was
not seen to be very interesting. After all it was written
by a peasant, a madman, a person who committed crimes
against nature. Thus it could serve only as a forensic
document, evidence for what the discourses of the contending powers, the judge, the lawyers, the police, and
the psychiatrists, wished to prove.[132]

And yet, it was strange that this madman, this village
idiot whom the papers called a *furieux*, could write forty
pages of lucid (though often ungrammatical) prose, whose
memoir led to a hung jury, an appeal, and a long debate on
Esquirol's recent linguistic invention, homocidal mono-
mania, in the pages of learned journals. That is, Rivière's
document was a full-fledged (though defeated) contestant in
the struggle of power-knowledge fought over and around him
by the learned. Pierre Rivière was an author. His discourse
was full of detail because it was an attempt to raise the
daily and ordinary to the level of a text, an *oeuvre*. Once
it had become a text, a piece of writing, literature, it
was no longer just a wierd gesture but a part of history,
the same history that included Napoleon and the conquest
of Algeria, which Rivière also mentioned. The history to
which Rivière gained access includes, besides Napoleon,
and Napoleon's friends and enemies, peasants, thieves,
cannibals, madmen, and people who kill their pregnant

mothers. What bound them together was murder. Napoleon,
the soldier, killed and risked death for glory; murderers
kill and risk execution for glory as well, for recognition,
for an end to resentments, for justice. This was why
accounts of murders were and are so popular: for sensa-
tional journalism, the bloodier and more unusual the
better. For murder mysteries, with their overlay of
bourgeois intellectualism, the more devious and clever
the better. Edmund Wilson once asked: "who gives a
damn who killed Roger Ackroyd." Lots of people, evidently.
The huge success of this kind of discursive practice, which
has existed steadily from the nineteenth century, "manifests the desire to know and to recount how men were able
to ply themselves against power, to flout the law, to be
exposed to death by means of death."[133] This ambiguous
existence of murder and stories about murder reflected a
double dialectic: the right to kill and be killed, the
right to speak and tell stories. It was no more than the
initial glory of Achilles, the doer of great deeds (mostly
loosening the knees of other human beings and causing them
to find black death) and the speaker of great words (mostly
bragging of his great deeds). For Pierre Rivière and his
kind, the stories were generally told in song (as did
Homer) and in the first person. The criminal celebrated
his crime, accepted his guilt and the penalty he must pay.
He sang between two deaths: his own and the ones he killed.
This was what Pierre Rivière's memoir did as well. "There
is hardly any reason to doubt that Rivière undertook his crime
at the level of a certain discursive practice and knowledge
to which he was tied. He was *really* playing within the
inextricable unity of his parricide and his text; the legal
system, the system of murder-and-memoir, all formed another
ensemble called a 'criminal record'."[134] It would seem that
a majority of the jury found it more monstrous than mad that
Rivière should have played his own bloody game, a double

game in the text as well as the gesture, as author as well
as subject. Perhaps Rivière did not lose so badly after
all. The very silence in which his memoir was buried for
so long was also mute testimony to the power of his discourse to upset the smooth processes of control being put
in place by medico-legal practice.

PUNITIVE SYSTEMS

9

In 1972 Foucault gave a series of lectures on social control and punitive systems in nineteenth-century France. It was part of a larger project, "to follow the formation of certain types of knowledge on the basis of the juridico-political matrices that have given birth to them and that serve to support them." The hypothesis of power-knowledge was explicitly formulated: power was not an obstacle to knowledge nor were the two related simply as interests and ideologies. The problem was not only to discover how power used knowledge for its own ends or suppressed it in favour of something else. Power was finally seen as productive, "No knowledge is formed without a system of communication, of record-keeping and record-collection, or without replacing prior knowledge, which is in itself a form of power and is tied in its existence and its functioning to other forms of power. On the other hand, no power is exercised without the extraction, appropriation, distri-bution, or retention of knowledge. At this level there is not knowledge on one side and society on the other, or science on one side and the state on the other, but rather the fundamental forms of power-knowledge."[135] The configuration or form of power-knowledge in industrial society was the examination; it was the instrument for exclusion, punishment, and control. In the ancient polis it was measure that established order among men, between men and nature, and also defined mathematical and physical knowledge. In the middle ages, the investigation verified facts, events, acts, and rights, but also was the matrix that defined empirical knowledge of nature. In contrast,

the modern examination was the means to establish or restore
a norm, rule, division, qualification or exclusion, but also
it was the framework of all psychologies, psychoanalysis,
sociology--in short, all the social sciences. There was, of
course, some overlap. Generally speaking, however, each
served a distinctive function and was tied to a specific
political power: measure to a function of order, investigation to a function of centralization, examination to a
function of selection and exclusion.

   Medieval practice moved from revenge to punishment,
from accusation to investigation, from injury that led to
litigation to infraction that determined consequences, from
decision as proof to judgement as proof, from trial by combat
to trial by testimony. All of which was tied to the birth of
a state that increasingly confiscated the administration of
penal justice. In this way the judicial investigation came
into being, with its characteristic questions (who did what?
who says so? what is the evidence? how is it supported?),
and procedures (to establish facts, assess guilt and responsibility, determine the circumstances of the act), and with
characteristic actors as well--prosecutors, defendants,
accusers, witnesses for and against, judges. "This
judicial model of investigation rests entirely on a system
of power; it is this system that defines what must be constituted as knowledge--how, from whom and by whom it is
extracted, in what way it is shifted about and transmitted,
at what point it is gathered together and leads to a judgement or a decision."[136] From the sixteenth century this
model was transformed by the empirical sciences and gave
rise to a new literary genre, the analytical investigation,
as distinct from the essay, the meditation, or the treatise.
But these later transformations were variations on a continuing theme. Modern civilization was essentially an
investigative one: it extracted, combined, and accumulated
knowledge. The truth of experiment and of experience was

the offspring of investigation: political, administrative
and judicial power asked questions, got answers, gathered
evidence, supervised statements and established facts just
as in ancient Hellas the truth of measure and proportion
was the offspring of *dike*. This was true for the extreme
form of repression and punishment that existed in the prison
as well as in the diffuse policing and spiritual direction
that was found in non-legal power, and that went by the
name of common decency.

In 1975 Foucault published *Surveiller et punir*.[137] A
few years later in a round-table discussion with a number
of historians knowledgeable in nineteenth-century things,
he explained what he had tried to do. He was not studying
a period, he said, but a problem; he had tried to argue that
the way things have turned out was not inscribed by some
mysterious necessity. "It is in no way evident that madmen
must be recognized as mentally ill; nor that the only thing
to do with a delinquent is to lock him up; nor that the
causes of illness be sought for in an individual examination
of the body."[138] Mental illness, prisons, and clinical
medicine are specific innovative responses to madness,
crime and illness. In particular, modern prisons express
discontinuities with the old regime both as regards their
ostensible purpose, and their actual techniques and consequences.

Generally speaking, four kinds of punishment have been
used in western societies. Classical Greek and Roman
citizens could suffer exile, banishment, exclusion from
certain areas, confiscation of property or destruction of
their homes. The antique Germanic tradition practiced
compensation, atonement and fines as the chief method.
Third, the marks of power may be inscribed directly on
one's body by branding, wounding, or mutilation, as in
the late middle ages and the old regime. And lastly, there
was jail. Prior to the activities of the penal reformers

during the period between 1780 and 1820, jails were used
for other reasons, for the safekeeping of prisoners who
could be ransomed, to protect public morality or to correct
immorality. It was, no doubt, all very unpleasant:
repression is hardly a modern innovation. Yet, a turning-
point in the history of repression did mark the transition
from the old regime: "it was seen to be more effective
and cheaper, according to the economy of power, to keep
watch over people rather than punish them. This moment,
which was at once rapid and slow, signals the formation of
a new kind of exercise of power during the eighteenth
century and the beginning of the nineteenth."[139]

   There was a change, first, in the relation of the
visible to the invisible. Publicity would attend the trial,
not the execution of the sentence. The theatrical and
spectacular aspect of punishment was suppressed and reversed:
not rituals of dismemberment but the brooding presence of
high prison walls would be the modern manifestation of
punishment. Punishment became abstract, not immediate; it
would deter by being certain, not horrible. A second major
axis of change: the body was no longer central. Bodies
would no longer be hurt, but were simply the means of access
to the judicial person and his rights, which were to be
suspended. The objective was not the body but the soul, so
that motives were as important as actions, if not more so.
Punishment, accordingly, would not efface the crime but
transform the (actual or potential) criminal. When this
was deemed impossible, in cases of capital crimes, punishment would be carried out upon bodies that, usually, would
be heavily tranquilized. This is also why it has become
important to establish an affinity between criminal and
crime, to create a non-corporal unit whose inner biography
would be the index of his reformation. The change, that
is, was from physical confrontation to intellectual struggle.
There was less violence but deeper intervention, and a

tendency to medicalize crime. Sustaining the changed
relations of visible and invisible, of body and soul, was
the new, modern social order.

Following the French Revolution new threats and new
illegal practices came into existence for which new laws
and new techniques of power were required. The Revolution
showed that a political order could be overthrown, but more
importantly, the new economic regime needed stability and
regularity if it were to function. In cities, large amounts
of goods were gathered together and so could be pillaged;
thus, if factories and industries were to work, this capital
investment must be protected, which meant guarding docks,
ports, arsenals, and factories. In the countryside the
exactly opposite social event produced the same result:
when a small number of large landowners gave way to a large
number of small farmers, that is, when rural capital was
diffused rather than concentrated, then minor illegalities
could no longer be tolerated. No more vagrants, no more
bandits, no more poachers, no more smugglers; obligations
would be enforced by a finer web of power. The slippage
and tolerance of the old regime was replaced by the assiduous
application of the law. This was marked in popular lore by
the disappearance of heroic, brave, criminal celebrities.
Only under very unusual circumstances has even the image
survived (in the wild west, Chicago gangland of the 1930's,
Bonnie and Clyde). In the modern era, the criminal acted
against society not the king; thus, the king did not avenge
himself, society protected itself, and the interests of
society must be served by punishment. This has had several
consequences.

First, each society must devise its own punishments
since the harm comes not from the act itself but from the
damage done to society. There is no universal model, so
that a weak society must exact severe penalties. Second,
if penalties were expiations, there are some crimes for

which no penalty could be sufficient. These are what Kant
called instances of radical evil. But if protecting society
was what is involved, it must be regulated by an economy of
offence and punishment: all acts can be mechanically graded
in accordance with the threat they pose to society. Punishment must fit not only the crime but the criminal. Third,
punishment was external and was directed towards the future
so as to ensure it was not repeated: in the end, the last
crime would not be punished. This was called humanitarianism.

The triumph of humanitarian incarceration was accompanied
by a great debate. Conservative critics who upheld the
virtues of the existing legal traditions maintained that
prisons would diminish the power of the judiciary to regulate
and verify the execution of penalties: the law did not enter
prisons but, precisely, was suspended, along with the rights
of citizens, in favour of rules and internal administrative
decrees. Others said that, by mixing up different kinds of
condemned persons, a homogeneous community of criminals
would be created, a veritable army of internal enemies who
later would be let loose on society. What was worse, by
providing the condemned with food and lodging, society
risked encouraging the lazy to become criminals. In reply
it was said that the only alternative was the penal colony
and France had too few of these. Moreover, the system could
be reformed so it wouldn't produce enemies of society.
Prisons would become penitentiaries. Prisoners would be
partially or completely isolated so as to reform their
conscience; they would be morally educated through labour,
instruction, exhortation, religion, rewards for good
behaviour, and so on; preventative para-penal institutions
would be established to prevent recidivism through controlled supervisions.[140] And governing all this, providing
it with the promise of certainty and success was the new
science of criminology. The anthropological status of
criminals and delinquents could be precisely defined in

terms of their psycho-sociological deviance. Correspondingly,
the existence of an incarcerated population would provide the
subject-matter for scientific discussion. Thus one again
found a conjunction of power and knowledge equal in convenience to that which brought the mentally ill and the
psychiatrists into their joyless embrace.

The triumph of the penitential prison was not the result
of humanitarian breezes blowing through the corridors of
nineteenth-century power. Nor did it have much to do with
the obvious good sense of the reformers' opinions. Rather,
their new truths had an affinity to other new truths, their
kind of incarceration and containment had an affinity with
other, equally effective, configurations of power that had
existed from as early as the seventeenth century and whose
roots were thoroughly medieval.[141] First of all, persons
had been concentrated or spatially dispersed for a long time.
Beggars and vagabonds had been periodically cleaned out of
cities and sent off to the countryside to work, particularly
during harvests. Moreover, the objective was correct
behaviour and ensuring order rather than moral reform or
strict obedience to the law: "The irregular, the agitated,
the dangerous, and the infamous were the objects of containment. Whereas penalties punished infractions, containment
dealt with disorder."[142] Even though outside judicial
control, the operations of *lettres de cachet* was not simply
the exercise of arbitrary political power. Most were
requests by parents to get rid of delinquent children or
by citizens to get rid of bothersome neighbours. That
is, there already existed a mechanism of local control:
requests went up from below and royal decrees came back
down. The innovation brought about by the Revolution was
to adjust the function of the judicial system so that it
became an integral part of the new *dispositif* of surveillance and supervision.[143]

This new array of institutional power, with prisons

at the top and other areas of containment scattered through
society in the form of charitable societies, orphanages,
apprenticeships, schools, and trade unions, was complimented
by a new knowledge. In the seventeenth century, for example,
soldiers were born, not made; by the late eighteenth century
they were made--by discipline, by the calculated manipu-
lation of the gestures and behaviour of bodies. This was
achieved by a minute attention to detail, first of all by
defining a separate space, a barracks, a school, a factory,
or a prison, that would be functionally articulated according
to rank. The result was a kind of administrative table.
Next, activity would be controlled according to a pre-
arranged sequence, a time-table; bodies would be programmed
to behave in one way and not another; gestures would be
learned along with the proper way to relate to objects
(rifles, machines, etc.); there would be no idleness, time
would be completely used up. Training would take place over
a definite period and would end with an examination. The
trained individual would be completely characterized both
with respect to others and with regard to his goal; he would
be well exercised, well practiced; accordingly, he would
react correctly to signals rather than explain to himself
what he was doing.[144] In other words, the changes in
punishment between 1760 and 1840 had less to do with the
nature of infractions (except that religious offences were
replaced with economic ones), than with the new significance
of the body and material things. A new kind of contact
began between human beings and their equipment, between
machinery and what made it go; new demands were placed on
individuals, on their bodies, as productive forces. The
history of prison reform, then, was part of the history of
the body rather than of morality.

Prisons were important because the body was no longer
to be mutilated but trained and retrained; its time must be
measured and fully used; its force continually applied to

labour. "The form of prison for punishment corresponded to
the form of salary for labour." So too did medicine, the
science of bodily functions, become central to prison
practice: "Punishment must have curing as its goal."[145]
The prison was "the last figure in this age of discipline"
and simply the most extreme technique of finely tuned day-
to-day power over the body.[146] That technique of curing,
dressage, and discipline altered the relations of bodies
and power. The old methods of constraint, supervision and
adjustment were simply and immediately corporal. The new
ones were material without being corporal, and operated
according to the laws of optics and mechanics.[147] The
central feature of the new optics was generalized and
constant surveillance. Everything must be observed, monitored, and transmitted to a police organization, the heart
of which was a system of archives with individual entries.
The ideal, no doubt, was an ingenious device, thought up
by members of the Okhrana who worked in the "Secret Room,"
of a very large sheet of paper where any "subversive" could
be exhaustively socio-grammed.[148] Nowadays large sheets of
paper have been replaced by the clever murmur of computers.
In harmony with the new optics was a new mechanics.
Individuals were to be isolated and regrouped; bodies
would be organized so as to be efficient; output would
be supervised. In short, life, time, and energy would all
be disciplined. And finally, there was a new physiology.
Norms were to be defined and what failed to conform would
be excluded and rejected. That is, a *dispositif* of
intervention was established to serve both therapeutic
and punitive purposes. "The power of normalization imposes
homogeneity; but it individualizes by making it possible
to measure gaps, to determine levels, to fix specialities
and to render differences useful by fitting them one to
another."[149] In this way it both presupposes equality
and justifies differences or inequalities.

   The examination, which Foucault earlier had identified
as the form of power-knowledge in industrial society,
combined observational hierarchy with normalization. In
hospitals, schools, and the army, as well as in prison,
disciplinary power was uninterrupted and continuous, but
also invisible rather than glorious. Military parades,
for example, became reviews not triumphal marches. Homogeneous meanings may be provided by files, dossiers, and
archives that can be encoded for quick retrieval of
information. Individuals become "cases," objects of
knowledge and things over which power could therefore be
exercised. Accordingly, there could be no heroes. In
the old regime individuality could appear at the top in
all its glory; in the new one it appeared at the bottom
in all its detail. Or rather, there was no top or bottom
so much as a multi-dimensional field surveyed by an all-
penetrating scan.

   The great virtue of panopticism was that it regularized
and homogenized. The motives in the observers in Bentham's
device counted for as little as those of the observed: what
made it work were the optical and mechanical laws built into
its architecture. Moreover, it could be expanded from its
locus in the distinctive space of prison or school to society
at large. Discipline would no longer be only a means to
neutralize danger but could become the purpose of society.
A disciplined society was useful, efficient and productive.
And it was accompanied by a vast increase in the amount of
information collected by the state so as to monitor and
control the general population. That is, discipline itself
was a technology of power. It enabled human beings to be
accumulated, organized, and set to work the way earlier
economists had spoken of capital. Discipline mediated
universality and particularity by translating universal
judicial norms, the rule of law, and so forth into correct
behaviour. In Foucault's words, Bentham's panopticon

"represented the abstract formula of a very real technology,
that of individuals."[150]   Combined with discipline and
normalization, panopticism institutionalized the new power
over the body. Like the psychological subject discussed
earlier, the body could become an object of knowledge; it
could be trained, could deviate and become pathological,
but could be normalized again too. It was the necessary
complement to the psychological subject. The indefinite
segmentation of a few spectacular criminal bodies pulled
apart in public executions dissolved, in the modern age,
into the indefinite interrogation of many bodies under
constant observation.

     One of the criticisms raised by conservative opponents
of the penitentiary movement, as was mentioned above, was
that, by concentrating a criminal population together for
a long period of time, a population of delinquents would
be created. And, in fact, during the classical age there
were no delinquents because there was no marination of them
within the system, no micro-society where men could develop
the solidarity necessary to constitute their delinquency.
The production of delinquents by prison experience has
persistently been seen as one of its most persistent
failures. All programmes for reform from the mid-nineteenth
century on have proposed the same things and affirmed the
same purposes, a complex of architecture and discourse,
coercive regulation and scientific proportion, real social
effects and invincible utopias, programmes to correct
delinquency and mechanisms to reinforce it.[151]   But in
the event, "from the moment when someone entered prison,
a mechanism was put into operation that would make him
infamous; and when he left he could become nothing but
a delinquent . . . . The prison professionalized."[152]
Prisoners learned nothing useful while sitting in jail
or performing hard labour, and they were burdened with a
record when they got out. That is, far from obliterating

the crime, time in jail conferred a new status that would
endure until the individual died. Delinquency, then, has
become a mechanism of repression.

But if that is the case, it is wrong or at least very
misleading to think that prisons have failed. One should
ask, rather, what purposes were served by the production of
a delinquent population. Certainly there were no more nomadic
gangs roaming the countryside in savage freedom. Modern
criminals have become urbanized. So, generally, were the
poor and the proletarian, since capital goods have generally
been located in cities. Moral teachings can only go so far
in protecting this property. Terror, or at least the threat
of violence, has also been required. A pervasive atmosphere
of fear is now provided by the non-moral, the bad, and the
delinquent. They have become a danger not so much to the
rich as to the poor, the good poor, who are the working
poor. These people presently live in families, hold jobs
and so on, but also read tabloid newspapers full of lurid
details about shocking crimes, which reinforces the image
of danger produced by the delinquent class. That is, the
poor offer up a section of themselves as delinquents who
then could terrify the remainder.[153] Prisons are simply
the instruments of recruitment.

If delinquents have provided the image of fear, the
police have provided the substance. Together they have
operated upon the restive elements of industrial society.
"Without delinquents, no police. Who would endure a police
presence, what makes a police administration tolerable if
not fear of the delinquent? . . . . If we accept in the
midst of us these men in uniform, armed when we do not
have the right to be, who ask to see our identification
papers, who hang around the streets--how would that be
possible without delinquents? And if there were not
newspaper stories appearing every day telling us how
numerous and dangerous delinquents were."[154] The

symbiotic relations between police and delinquents has had
certain direct benefits for the police as well: controlled
illegality can be very profitable. Prostitution, for example,
or bootlegging or drug trafficking have all become more or
less regulated by the police because of the semi-clandestine
nature of the pleasures they involve, which inevitably results
in high prices. All expensive things must be protected.
There are fringe benefits as well, in the form of lower
wages, availability of strike-breakers, spies and pro-
vocateurs, etc., but these goods generally do not accrue
directly to the police.

The other identifiable group who have directly benefitted
by the production of delinquents have been, naturally enough,
the criminologists, penologists, and prison "reformers."
Their discourse has been almost entirely utilitarian; its
ostensible purpose has been to justify the act of transforming men, not punishing them. Without a steady stream
of delinquents to study, the discourse of the penologists
would dry up; they would lack a subject upon which to
practice their ever-refined science. At present, this seems
hardly likely to occur since prisons are, if anything,
bursting with subject-matter, with objects for study. But
this, too, is to the advantage of criminologists since now
they are called upon to invent new techniques of supervision
and exclusion that will enable some of those inside to come
out but still be controlled. Nothing significant is changed
if delinquents are under the surveillance of psychiatrists
rather than thugs--except, perhaps that the aggression is
more subtle. Valium is more effective on some people than
truncheons.

Delinquents, then, have played a significant role in
the surveillance of society. They have provided secret
agents and their presence has authorized generalized
policing. Categorized by their relationship to penal
institutions, they have become preeminently the excluded

sector of modern society. They are irregular to the extent
that their behaviour is illegal. Or rather, their illegality should be seen not as a kind of accident or more or
less inevitable imperfection in the otherwise smooth operation
of society, but as an absolutely essential element. So, in
answer to the question, why prisons? Foucault suggested that
an answer may be found along the following lines: "prison
has the advantage of producing delinquents, the instruments
of supervision and repression of illegality, a not negli-
gible element in the exercise of power over bodies, an element
in that physics of power that has also produced the psychology
of the subject."[155] Prisons have become the centre of a network of power: they are the strong end of a carcereal
continuum that extends via reformatories and schools, trade
unions and social workers, universities and corporations and
hospitals, throughout society. In the following section the
infiltration of power in society is discussed. To conclude
this account of punitive systems of power, a few words on
Foucault's immediately polemical activities are in order.

In the wake of a series of prison strikes and revolts
during the fall and winter of 1971, Foucault, along with
Pierre Vidal-Naquet and Jean-Marie Domenach created the
Group d'Information sur les Prisons, the G.I.P. Originally
they had four basic objectives, to ensure that the labour
done by inmates was useful training for when they were
released, to obtain legal protection for inmates, to gain
inmates the right to discuss prison conditions on the outside, and to ensure that criminal records would be destroyed
when convicts were released, thus ending their status as
delinquents.[156] The G.I.P. published a few pamphlets
on prison conditions, on the methods of control, including
an autobiographical questionnaire that inmates are required
to answer, but their main activity was to sponsor discourse. "The G.I.P. does not presume to speak for those
detained in various prisons: it proposes, on the contrary,

to give them the possibility of speaking themselves, and to
tell what goes on in prison. The goal of the G.I.P. is not
reformist, and we do not dream of an ideal prison: we would
like the prisoners to be able to say what is intolerable in
the system of penal repression. We have a duty to dissemin-
ate as quickly and as widely as possible revelations made by
the prisoners themselves. It is the only way to unite those
inside and those outside in the same struggle."[157] More
broadly, Foucault has said that the goal of the G.I.P. "was
not to extend the visiting rights of prisoners to thirty
minutes or to procure flush toilets for the cells, but to
question the social and moral distinction between the
innocent and the guilty."[158] A book that fulfilled both
objectives was Serge Livrozet's *De la prison à la revolte*.

It was an unusual kind of prison memoir, Foucault said,
because it contained ideas. Normally one expects only to
read about all the unhappy events and bad luck that led the
hapless victim to a lamentable life of crime. "The
infraction was not undertaken in order to be thought about;
it must only have been lived, then recalled. We do not
tolerate anything systematic; nothing more than the simple
memory of the crime."[159] That was also why the criminal
has always been seen as a single individual: there could
be no collectivity or ensemble of criminal life, no honour
among thieves, nothing resembling a community with its own
standards. Indeed, the only plurality that criminals could
possess was that constituted by expert discourse, where
they became "deviants," the result of a series of mis-
fortunes, a possessive mother, a drunken father, an under-
developed superego, a broken home. It was all a matter
of statistical improbabilities. Livrozet's book, like
Rivière's memoir, was a form of struggle against the
exclusion of his thought by the imposition of external
norms and alien criteria about what was to count as
"knowledge."

In addition to writing about, and demonstrating against, police illegalities, illegal deportations, and murders by prison guards, Foucault has also written against the death penalty.[160] "Prison," he wrote, "is the only place where power is manifested in its naked state, in its most excessive form, and where it is justified as moral force . . . . What is fascinating about prisons is that, for once, power doesn't hide or mask itself; it reveals itself as tyranny pursued into the finest details; it is cynical at the same time pure and entirely 'justified,' because its practice can be totally formulated within the framework of morality. Its brutal tyranny consequently appears as the serene domination of Good over Evil, of order over dis-order."[161] At the summit of penal power is the guillotine and death. "The entire penal system is in the end oriented towards death and is governed by that end."[162] Even if given a jail sentence and not death, one has been put into a position where, eventually, one would be tempted by death. Prisons have become, if not suicide-machines, at least environments severe enough to induce the possibility of suicide as a way of dealing with the difficulties of living under such conditions.[163] Prison has become a theatre where death is always the centre of fascination. "Think about this: in prison you are punished when you attempt to kill yourself; and when prison is allowed to punish you fully, you are killed."[164] If the law were supposed to be correctional not punitive, then the death penalty made no sense. If the law said: stealing results in one hand being chopped off and rape gets you castrated, then it would make sense for murder to be balanced by a sentence of death. So long as the law is supposed to be "correctional," the death sentence is absurd.

Although Foucault has several times stated that he did not think it his task to provide alternatives to the systems he described because "to imagine another system is to extend our participation in the present system,"[165] there were some implications that, without a great deal of interpretative ingenuity, could be understood as obvious reforms. First of all, there was no reason to respect the guards as "defenders of society." They were, on the contrary, part of the same system of repression that included the army and the police. In a fine polemical piece, Foucault observed that they did have certain difficulties inasmuch as they belonged to the C.G.T., the Communist confederation of unions, and so to an organization that was "by definition" revolutionary.[166] Secondly, there were reasons to be sympathetic to the role of judges. Their task was to render justice not simply as a sovereign decree but also as a public service. But how could one take public service seriously when the institution of justice had as its most visible function the sentencing of people to death? "If a judge is a man who can cut you in two, he will not be recognized as the superintendent of public service."[167] Their dilemma was not simply public, however. There was an inherent problem in combining judges' independence of one another with the need for the law to be consistently applied, interpreted, and executed.

But these were just surface problems, occasions for the display of Foucault's wit and polemical talents. The role of the judge was to say the least, ambiguous. He stood between two systems of law, the old one, which demanded punishment, and the new, which envisaged therapy worked upon the social body. Thus, the law asked psychiatry three very strange questions—in addition to the traditional one, was the accused crazy? First: was he dangerous? Second, could he be influenced by penal sanctions? Third, was he curable or adaptable? "Three questions that have no judicial meaning. The law has never claimed to punish somebody because he is 'dangerous,' but because he is criminal. On the psychiatric level there is no meaning either: 'danger' is not a psychiatric category. No more

than the concept of 'adaptibility.'"[168] This strange mixture
of discourse may be reduced to the question of a danger for
society, which notion has neither a psychiatric nor a legal
meaning, but simply was a matter of power. In any case
psychiatrists could not turn delinquents into non-delinquents
and have never had any way of knowing if crime was an illness.
All the interventions of psychiatrists have done is relieve
the anxiety of judging. But why should it not be increased?
What right have judges to judge? in whose name? and who are
they to judge? That such questions might be disturbing to
judges is a triviality. Think how they disturb the ones they
judge. A terrible example of the psychiatrization of judging
and the relief from anxiety it has brought to judges was
provided by the case of a man, Christian Ranucci, who was
guillotined on July 28, 1976 after having confessed to murder.
The confession was not very precise, did not account for all
the facts, and was contradicted by other testimony. The
examining psychiatrist knew that Ranucci was guilty; he had
found a "criminal psyche" for which the act of murder
"naturally" followed. So the focus was no longer on an
obscure crime and uncertain facts but on the criminal and
his confession; here was a danger to society, a monster
who slaughtered an innocent little girl, and he was the
object on trial. "A paradox: one of the most solid roots
today surrounding the death penalty is the modern, humanitarian, scientific principle whereby one judges not crimes
but criminals. It is economically less costly, intellectu-
ally easier, more comfortable for judges and for public
opinion, more reasonable in the eyes of the wise, and more
satisfying for one's passions to 'understand the man' rather
than establish the facts."[169] And that was how one fine
morning justice cut into two pieces a "criminal" of twenty-
two years of age without having proved the crime.[170]

DOMESTICATION AND NORMALIZATION

10

The supreme expression of domestic state power is the
judicial right of execution. Justice, if it means anything
in a modern society, is judicial practice. It takes the form
of a tribunal and is to be contrasted with other kinds of
justice, specifically, with popular justice. Popular
justice is revoltuionary justice, justice unmediated by
tribunals or the state and so always closely bound to war
and retribution. Penal justice or state justice was created
along with the administrative centralization of armed and
unarmed bureaucracy. That is, the judiciary was an expression of public power coeval with the army and tax-collectors.
It was "an arbiter that was both neutral and authoritative,
charged with resolving litigation 'justly' at the same time
as assuring 'authoritatively' the maintenance of public
order."[171] The disposition of personnel in a tribunal
already implies the conjunction of power and knowledge:
a barrier separates the judicial from the public space;
the litigants are seated before the elevated dias on which
the judge sits; the jury sit to the side. The jury are
neutral with respect to the litigants; their judgement is
not determined in advance but only after listening to the
two parties and deliberating in light of the facts presented, a certain norm of truth (perhaps unspecified), and
a number of ideas about what is just and unjust. Their
judgement, generally speaking, is authoritative. The
configuration of neutrality, truth, and norms of justice
is in great contrast with the model of popular justice:
there one finds the populus and their enemies, not three
elements, one of which is guided by ideas. When one is

seen to be an enemy and is punished or re-educated, it is
not with reference to universal notions of justice but to
the immediate experiences of the populus. Their acts are
not authoritative in that they bear no reference to any
overarching legitimacy but are simply carried out. And,
of course, popular justice is vigorously denounced as an
abuse, as a violation of "true" justice, as a perversion
of "true" principles of jurisprudence, and so forth.[172]
All of which means no more than that popular justice is not
penal justice but that it is being judged according to the
standards of penal justice.

But, as has been indicated in the previous section,
penal justice has its own shadow inasmuch as it is part of
a general system of repression. During the middle ages,
repression was essentially a military operation. It was
succeeded by a complex system of justice-police-prison that
served a threefold function. It was an important factor in
"proletarianization," in inducing and constraining people
to accept their status as proletarian by providing them with
a worse alternative, jail. Hence the laws mentioned earlier
against begging, vagrancy, vagabonds, etc. Second, the
judicial-penal system operated especially against the
"natural" leaders of the plebians, the most mobile and
"violent," that is, courageous, persons who were likely to
resort to armed rebellion. Dispossessed peasants, bandits,
unemployed manual labourers became "dangerous" persons and
were sent to the colonies, the Hôpital Général, the galleys,
the workhouse, or to prison. And lastly, these non-
proletarian plebians were made to appear to the proletarians
as marginal, dangerous, immoral, and threatening. Hence the
assiduous use of a propaganda that told of universal norms
of justice and morality, and that were backed by scientific
accounts of criminality and deviance. Historically the state
used, in addition to the judicial-penal system, the army and
the police as a means of enrolling one fraction of plebians

to repress the rest. Peasants in the army could be given
colonial duties where they would be educated to be racists,
not proletarians, or to jail where they could learn to be
delinquents. With the recent decolonization movements,
the role of the army has sadly been diminished; but that
also meant that the judicial-prison system has been given
an enhanced significance. The consequence of this elaborate
recruitment, according to Foucault, was to maintain a docile
proletariat, lacerated by internal social divisions and
afraid of its own violence. "Penal justice was not produced
by the plebians, nor by the peasantry, nor by the proletariat,
but quite simply by the bourgeoisie as an important tactical
instrument in the system of divisions that it sought to
introduce."[173] The penal system, then, is not a vague
ideological superstructure nor is it the embodiment (however
imperfect) of universal norms of truth and justice. It has
become the great bulwark against "subversion" and, by that
title, is also the most important expression of contemporary
power and order, the chief means to maintain the existing
divisions within society.

Not all power is legal power and not all social divisions
are maintained by the judicial-penal system. Prison is the
last resort of power and its *ultima ratio*. More to the point,
however, both the ultimate source of state power and the
thinner, more diffuse webs of power that regulate and
normalize, are all organized by a political knowledge
centred on the notion of a population and mechanisms
designed to ensure its management. This is the modern
meaning of "government."

The government of men is "an activity that undertakes
to direct individuals throughout their life by placing them
under the authority of a guide who is responsible for what
they do and what happens to them."[174] It is a notion quite
foreign to classical Greek political thought, even as an
account of the actions of the *nomothete*; it appeared there

only to describe the activities of teachers, physicians, and gymnastics masters. The political "sovereign-pastor" is an oriental symbol, ultimately a Pharonic attribute, which was transmitted to the west by Israelite and espec- ially Christian religious experience. The power of the "shepherd" was exercised less within a fixed territory than over a multitude that was directed towards a specific goal. He provided the daily bread and assured salvation; he cared as much for the individual lamb as for the entire flock. "This is the type of power introduced into the west of Christianity; it has taken the institutional form of an ecclesiastical pastorate. The governance of souls is con- stituted in the Christian Church as a central and salvific activity, indispensable to the salvation of each and all."[175] From the general crisis in pastoral relations that was marked by the protestant reformation, a new and more complex form of governance was created, which was based on new economic and social relations and had as its objective the spiritual direction of the family, children, the domain, kingdom, and in fact of the entire population. Indeed, the concept of a "population" arose from the necessity to control, preserve, and augment labour-power within the new industrializing states. People had to be watched, controlled, administered, and so on, but first they had to be identified correctly. Hence the new science of statistical demography, which was centred on bodies and bodily changes and mapped the world in terms of age, sex, usefulness, marriage ratios, and mortality rates. The change was greater than was indicated in Max Weber's argument about the secularization of Christian aescetic impulses. It was no less than a scientifically justified but nevertheless forced monasticization of the newly created "population" into various sorts of asylums: schools, factories, universities, barracks, and office buildings.[176]

Changes in political "governmentality," that is, in "the manner by which the conduct of an ensemble of individuals becomes integrated in increasingly obvious ways into the exercise of sovereign power,"[177] were indicated in the manner that the "art" that is, the technique, of government has been described. Emphasis on the traditional virtues (wisdom, justice, liberality, respect for divine laws and human traditions), or of practical traditions (prudence, reflection before deciding on a course of action, taking the advice of wise counsellors), gave way to an art whose rationality of principle and domain of application were specifically tied to the state. The notion of "raison d'état" was not an imperative in the name of which one can or must break all other rules; it was the new matrix of rationality according to which the prince must exercise his sovereignty in governing men. One may savour the irony that it was first formulated, perfected, and put into practice by the episcopal agents of Innocent III. More importantly, raison d'état entered the space left by the dissolution of the imperial and eschatological symbols of medieval Rome, the *sacrum imperium*. "A new historical perception is forming; it is no longer focussed on the end of time and the unification of all particularist sovereignties within the empire of the last days; it is open to an indefinite time when states have to struggle one against the other to ensure their own survival."[178] The sovereign's legitimacy became less important than the creation and augmentation of state forces within particular spaces that allowed the state to act. In this way were developed the two great technologies of modern politics, "a diplomatic-military technology that consists in maintaining and developing the forces of the state through a system of alliances and a machinery of armed forces; the quest for a European equilibrium, which was one of the directing principles of the Treaty of Westphalia, is a consequence of this

political technology. The other is constituted by the 'police'
in the sense of an ensemble of means necessary to make the
power of the state grow from within."[179] At the centre of
both was commerce and trade between states, which led to an
increase in population, export, and the size of armies. It
consolidated the concept of population-wealth at the centre
of government rationality.

The elaboration of the implications of population-wealth,
namely fiscal theory, scarcity, depopulation, beggary, and
vagrancy, constituted the condition for the creation of
political economy. The new science brought a means of control to a complex of resources and population that could not
be managed solely by means of coercion and quasi-military
rule. Political economy, that is, was a part of the technique
of police, born with reflection on the political-economic
problem of population. A population, in the modern sense,
is not a series of legal subjects nor a work force. It is
an analytical term that indicates an ensemble of elements
that, on the one hand, "are tied to the general regime of
living beings (the population is thus linked to the 'human
species,' a new term, and quite distinct from the 'human
genus'), and, on the other, to a justification for direct
intervention in its management (by the intermediary of laws,
but also by changes in attitude, of ways of acting and
living, which can be achieved by undertaking 'campaigns')."[180]
The modern activity of the police, which is, practically
speaking, the defining characteristic of a *state* (as
distinct from a bourgeois *society*), is one of internal
control by means of a general provision of "well-being"
for the population. Peace and tranquility, peace, order,
and good government, if you will, implied biopolitical
population management.

Here is encountered the division between premodern
and modern technologies of power. The former essentially
meant the appropriation of wealth, a tax of products, goods,

services, labour, and blood. "Power in this instance was
essentially a right of seizure: of things, time, bodies,
and ultimately life itself: it culminated in the privilege
to seize hold of life in order to suppress it."[181] No
longer. Now the technique of execution is relatively
unimportant and power is directed towards the controlled
generation of forces rather than their destruction. This
is why, as was argued earlier, the arguments for capital
punishment eventually fall back upon the danger to "society"
presented by real or potential killers and not upon the right
of the sovereign to annihilate enemies. Death and violence,
that is, are justified nowadays by the right of a population
to survive. "Entire populations are mobilized for the
purpose of wholesale slaughter in the name of life necessity:
massacres have become vital. It is as managers of life and
survival, of bodies and the race, that so many regimes have
been able to wage so many wars, causing so many people to be
killed."[182] And the final end-point has surely been reached
with atomic weapons, which expose the entire present population and thereby the potential of human generation as
such, to death. The danger of extinction is the underside
of the same technological power that is invoked as the
guarantee of an individual's continued existence. That
is, the life of the species has been wagered on its own
political strategy, which is the administration of bodies
and the calculated management of itself. The distance and
play opened up by ritual and law has gone: there is seldom
any reference to the sword and its swift and terrible acts.
Nothing is terrible any more. Instead there is a continuous
regulation of life. The task of power is "to qualify,
measure, appraise, and hierarchize, rather than display
itself in its murderous splendour; it does not have to
draw the line that separates enemies of the sovereign from
his obedient subjects; it effects distributions around the
norm."[183] Law as a whole has become administrative regu-

lation; our present normalized society is the historical
consequence of a technology of power centred upon life.
It has, moreover, been a great success, at least so far.
The power of the state and therefore of the police has
steadily grown.

To analyze power relations concretely, the judicial
model of sovereignty must be abandoned. It presupposes the
individual as a subject possessing natural rights or powers,
sees its task as accounting for the establishment of the
state, and sees law as the manifestation of power. In
addition to the elements of this theory, namely individuals
and the law, relations of subjection are created by other
techniques of constraint. Now, if power is primarily manifested as relations of force and will (whether personal or
quasi-anonymous) the question arises as to whether war
provides an adequate general model for the analysis of power-
relations. This leads to some further preliminary questions:
is war the most fundamental relationship so that domination
and hierarchy are derived from it? are class, group, and
individual struggles examples of this general process of
war? are notions derived from strategy and tactics useful
for the analysis of power-relations? and, first of all,
how is society fundamentally a battle, and when did people
start thinking that way?

The kind of discourse Foucault was concerned with to
answer such questions was not that of Hobbes or even
Mandeville, but of legal practitioners of political struggle,
Selden, Coke and Lilburn in England, Boulainvillers, Frevet,
and Buat-Nancay in France. Their historico-political (not
philosophico-juridical) discourse took place in a context
of power defined primarily by the concentration of war-
making capacities in a central authority and the emergence
of professional soldiers with their own techniques of
organization. Beginning with the sixteenth- and seven-
teenth-century wars of religion and political struggle, it

was argued that states were created by wars—not "ideal"
wars that took place *in illo tempore*, in a state of nature,
and so on, but by real wars. Moreover, war continued, within
the state, to be its secret animating force, what kept its
institutions effective and its laws obeyed. War "divided
the entire social body on a permanent basis; it placed each
of us in one camp or another. And this war was not simply
an explanatory principle; it was necessary to revive it, to
make it abandon its masked and mute forms (where it nevertheless continued) if it is to be properly understood and
we are to be prepared for victory in this most decisive
battle."[184]

From within this very general thematic space a few other
points may also be made. First, the speaker of such discourse
is not one who claims a position of universality. He is not
a jurist or a philosopher but a partisan: he upholds the
law, but it is his law, and it is maintained by conquest,
domination or tradition, which is to say race, triumphant
invasion, or long-term occupation. Truth, if it is mentioned,
is a strategic notion, a means to gain a victory. There is
no pretense to being above the fray: law is imposed and is
intended and designed to reflect and embody the privileges
of the victor. Universal truth and general justice are
illusions. Secondly, it is a discourse that overturns
traditional views of intelligibility: what explains things
is the lowest, the most confused, obscure, and open to
chance. Violence, hatred, passion, revenge, these are the
means to decipher events; they also constitute the tissue
of circumstance that brings victory or defeat. The shadowy,
slippery gods of war must somehow clarify the long days of
peace: brutal facts and luck must be controlled by the
only remaining rationality, that of calculation and
reckoning upon consequences. Moreover, even the rationality of calculation grew fragile as it succeeded: there
were always too many factors to be controlled, too many

temptations of illusion. "Here one finds the complete contrary
to those traditional analyses that tried to find under the
contingency of appearance and surface, under the visible
brutality of bodies and passions, a fundamental and permanent rationality that was essentially tied to the just and
the good."[185] On the contrary, nothing was taken to be
permanent, least of all the calculative rationality that tried
to impose order. Finally, then, this discourse of war was
entirely historical. It made no attempt to gauge history,
injustice, abuse, violence, terror, etc., by any principle or
law: it sought simply to reveal the forgotten past of struggle,
victory and defeat that lay behind laws and institutions. Even
though the field of reference was the uncertain movement of
history, it could at the same time be infused with a mythic
meaning, a heroic past for aristocrats, a glorious future for
proletarians. Both, however, could be actualized only by
victory; both, therefore, presupposed war.

      The conclusion to which one has been led is, then, that
the fundamental relationship in modern society is indeed
conflict, and that it is understood to be so by the founders
of modern society, that domination, by class or group or
individual, is essentially a strategic activity with no
transcending justification. It follows that, if the contemporary successors to modernity deny it or are scandalized by
their own heritage, this may be part of their cunning or it
may simply reflect their ignorance. But either way, the
analyst of power in modern society is justified in viewing
the consequences of their activity as the elaboration of a
strategy. Some of the elements of this strategy have been
presented in earlier sections and may be summarized under
three heads: first, there is a new optics, a generalized
organization of watching. Everything is to be monitored for
irregularities. Second, there is a new mechanics: individuals are to be separated (and even isolated) and regrouped
so as to achieve a specific and precise goal. All life is

to be disciplined. Third, there is a new physiology: norms
must be defined and the means of intervention established.
Bodies are to be managed and deviance corrected.

The extent of regularization and normalization envisaged by the original practitioners of the new police state
is indicated in a text mentioned above, Nicolas de La Mare's
Traité de Police.[186] Originally projected for twelve books,
only six were completed, the last by the hand of Cler du
Brillet. The final six books were to deal with public
security, science and liberal arts, commerce, manufacturing
and mechanical arts, servants both domestic and labouring,
and lastly, the poor. The existing six books are a compendium
of history and law. In addition they contain an elaborate
justification for supervision and regulation of all aspects
of public life. In the epistle dedicatory (to Louis XIV)
La Mare declared that the police were concerned with everything dealing with that good order upon which the happiness
of states depends. Indeed, by police "is meant the public
order of each city." Of particular significance is the care
of the poor which, he said, had no counterpart in ancient
times. If one considered their care to be part of charity,
it ought be studied under the head of religion. "But if
one attends to idleness, libertinage, and an infinity of
other vices of which poverty is the source and which can
be prevented, corrected, or punished only by putting an end
to beggary, one then would include this aspect of police
under the category of the discipline of manners."[187] Thus
the prohibition of beggary obliged the poor to enter upon
the order where Providence had placed them: the invalids
in hospitals "and the others to employment commensurate
with their birth, their state, and their strength." By
diminishing the number of idle persons, the state would
be furnished with a new source of labourers and artisans.
"Consequently it is true to say that this policing of the
poor includes all the other tasks and all the other

objectives of the public good, and that it deserves its own
special title."[188] With such a broad mandate as the public
good and with the evident need to repress the evil of
poverty, or rather, of the poor, police activity was nothing
less than a replacement for religion: "if religion were
properly observed, all the other tasks of the police would
be accomplished."[189] But, alas, religion was not properly
observed. Consequently the police must discipline the
social body, even to the extent of punishing sorcerers.[190]
More positively, the police must ensure health, "so
precious a good and yet at the same time so fragile that
man is in constant danger of losing it." The remedy was
police protection, the elimination of external dangers by
laws governing public security and of internal dangers by
laws promoting salubrity of the air, purity of water and
quality of food.[191] Discipline, supervision, regulation,
normalization, the promotion of well-being, prosperity and
public order--all the elements of a police utopia were in
place, at least in the register of knowledge, long before
the upheavals at the end of the eighteenth century. It
took longer to erect the institutions to actualize La Mare's
vision of good order.

   The great flaw in all bureaucratic structures designed
to ensure smooth administration is that they must be staffed
with whimsical humans. It would be so much more efficient
if one could create a structure that, as Alfred Krupp once
said, would run at maximum efficiency no matter who did
what job. Harold Geneen, in a similarly light mood, wished
for, and tried to actualize in ITT, a regime of "no surprises."
The earliest steps in that direction were taken by La Mare's
post-Revolution successors. Their initial efforts were
confined to prisons, hospitals, and urban planning, but
the impetus to regularize was boundless. By focussing on
the disposition of masonry one could all but eliminate the
unpredictability of human beings. In the new architecture,

the principles of regularization took concrete form.

Architecture, as other human activities, responds to
personal, social, and political needs. The nineteenth
century had new needs. The crude presentation of power
in cathedral, chateau, and fortress gave way to the similarly
overwhelming presence of prison, hospital, factory, and large-
scale urban development. But in addition, the effects of
power were required to circulate in increasingly narrow
streams, down to the single individual body and its gestures.
The grand theory was provided by Rousseau and Bentham. The
Rousseauist dream of the Revolutionaries was to create a
transparent society with nothing hidden and truth visibly
inscribed everywhere in daily life. No privileged royal
bodies could be cloaked in mystery; the shadows and darkness of convents, ignorance, superstition, the back rooms
where priests and monarchs hatched their plots and conspired,
all that was to be dispelled by the light of opinion, "a
mode of functioning where power would be exercised solely
as a result of the fact that things are known and people
are seen by a kind of immediate, collective and anonymous
vision. A power whose principle method of application is
opinion can never tolerate any areas of shadow."[192] Bentham
succeeded in organizing visibility in a machine where, in
principle, everybody could be watched, and eventually everybody
would keep tabs on everybody else. His panopticon was
utopian in its social implications--though not as an
architectural model for prisons in Rennes (France) or
Statesville (U.S.A.)--because he attributed a democratic
character to opinion and, in that way, declared opinion to
be just. Another nineteenth-century mechanism of power,
journalism, brought the utopian inadequacies of a politics
of opinion-observation to light.

It was, however, anything but a utopian structure of
power. "The architectural dream of Bentham became a
judicial and institutional reality under the Napoleonic

state, which then served as the model of all nineteenth-
century states . . . . We live in a panoptic society."[193]
There is no homogeneous network of control centred at the
top somewhere; that was the archaic model of the old regime.
Modern power can be entrusted to no one, since no one can
occupy the role that the king had in the old regime, namely
the source of power and justice. Necessarily the king was
trusted because his power was of God, in whom all trust
reposed. A bad king was either an accident or divine
punishment. "But nowadays the business going on with family,
medicine, psychiatry, psychoanalysis, school, justice, and
with children, does not homogenize them all but establishes
between them connections, reciprocities, complimentarities,
delimitations that assume that each maintains its own characteristic attributes up to a certain point."[194] When power
is a matter of cogs and gears, of a machine whose smooth
working depends on having everyone function in his place,
then there can be no absolute concentration of power in
a single person. Its entire principle is one of mistrust.
Modern power, one may say, is the circulation of mistrust.
Accordingly, power does not, in the present age, simply take
the form of law nor is there a unity of domination. On the
contrary, power expresses "the multiplicity of relations of
force immanent in the sphere in which they operate and which
constitute their own organizations; as the process which,
through ceaseless struggles and transformations, alters,
strengthens, or reverses them; as the support which these
relations of force find in one another, thus forming a
chain or system or, on the contrary, the disjunctions and
contradictions that isolate them from one another; and
lastly, as the strategies in which they take effect, whose
general design or institutional crystalization is embodied
in the state apparatus, in the formulation of the law, in
the various social hegemonies."[195] In other words, panopticism has become diluted as the shift from Bentham's

argument or knowledge solidified in the power of bureaucratic and functionally overlapping structures. But the
dilution was hardly a weakening: like chromium added to
iron, it made a frame of stainless steel. Two constituent
elements may be distinguished: the domestication of nature
and moralism. The goal, though not the result, was the
correction of abnormality.

     During the early nineteenth century, the term *habitat*
took on a more or less technical meaning that implied an
administrative space suitable for political intervention.
The environment could be reduced to a statistical profile,
uniform and homogeneous area organized and defined by public
laws, regulated and monitored by a specialized administration.
It was to be a readable space that could serve as a means of
division and control, a general codification that would be
transparent to the state but opaque for popular power. The
reaction to the cholera epidemics of mid-century showed that
the attitudes of the old regime were gone.[196] Life, conceived
in terms of the social ideal of health, displaced religious
sacralization of mortality and fulfilment by grace in death;
death was transformed from the appearance of nothingness
to a statistical entity a mortality rate, not destiny or
fate but a scandal and an abuse, an object of calculation
with no aura of transcendence. The mystery of life and
death, once it has been transposed into health, led inevitably to the appearance of an apparatus to promote health.
That is, salubrity became a goal of public policy. Functional,
utilitarian and generalized public works and public buildings
replaced visible, spectacular, ostentatious and local ones.

     Salubrity could be defined by norms and could be
actualized more easily than health. Moreover, it was made
apparent by the alteration of urban space. Changing the
shape of the urban fabric meant more than replacing narrow
crooked lanes with wide boulevards and numbered houses.
Subterranean volumes were also re-organized and pierced

with pipes. From the mid-nineteenth century to the present,
then, daily life was increasingly defined not by the circulation of the wind and its smells, the alteration of the
seasons or the passage of comets, but by technical or
quasi-mechanical arrangements designed to direct various
natural fluids so as to maintain the health of the population. Air and water were uncertain and corruptible fluids,
but also necessary ones. Thus they had to be properly
ordered and directed, which led to a technical and architectural solution to the genesis of illness or at least
to an environment lacking in salubrity. Removal of cemeteries from water supplies and airing out hospital corridors
would diminish the impact of bad air and foul water and at
the same time materialize medical space. A second alteration was implied: cities were surveyed in the obvious
sense that their shape was plotted upon a grid by surveyors;
but they were metaphorically surveyed as well in that cities
were viewed from the perspective of birds or angels. This
meant that the historical significance of any specific
piece of territory dissolved into utility, which auto-
matically made it fit for political alteration.[197] The
entire process may be understood as one of domestication not
simply in the sense of segregating the unpleasant consequences of the liberal domination of nature, but also in
the sense of introducing into the domestic, home, or
hitherto private space, the beneficent consequences of
the new technical attitudes. "Domestication of fluids
such as air, water, heat, light; domestication of practices
such as hygiene, family life, sexuality. Domestication of
these practices by way of those fluids, and of the fluids
by way of new measures and new equipment."[198] One can
imagine an entire and new domestic universe including
architecture but also gardening, waterworks, bathrooms,
stores, and nowadays electricity, radio, television,
telephones, garages, and, of course, air conditioning or

"climate control." Today, even the seasons can be eliminated.
Most of these things were not invented for household use but
were, precisely, domesticated.

Moralism in social life was the result of an alteration
in medical perception and of economic discourse. The old way
of talking about illness placed it in the context of a
specific etiology; likewise, economic discourse maintained
that poverty was also part of a specific causal sequence
that, in principle, could be suppressed. But the new medical
perception and the new political economy altered these
relations: clinical medicine was external to the old discourse that dealt with cause and effect and political
economy had nothing to say about illness. A new discourse
was created to deal not with the sick person, *le malade*, but
with *le misérable*. Strictly speaking, the new moralizing
or reformist discourse dealt neither with poverty nor
sickness. "It dealt with misery, but it strictly separated
it from poverty. It can handle the frequency of illness
and mortality, but in terms of a statistical discourse not
a medical one. Between poverty and misery a certain attitude
is inserted concerning labour, leisure, and money. Between
statistical frequencies and the poorer classes, a certain
attitude is inserted concerning the body, health, and
sickness. It is called the 'moral situation,' which is
joined soon enough by a concern for the 'physical situation,'
which does not refer to poverty but to the material frame
within which it is lived."[199] Four varieties of moralist
or reformist discourse were elaborated. One stressed the
evil consequences of bad air, dirty water, alcohol, etc.:
social pathology was not necessarily tied to any one class.
Alternatively there emerged a discussion of the material
life of the poor and its relation to the low level of their
moral life: a happy and disciplined poverty would emerge
from a change in their material circumstances. Thirdly,
the equation could be reversed: poverty and misery could

be distinguished, misery resulted from moral degeneration,
and reform meant moral uplift for, and of, but not necessarily by, the poor. Finally, there were utopian and revolutionary discourses that specified the link between poverty
and misery but for that reason also were burdened with the
task of calling the assumptions of political economy into
question.

The political correlate to the new discourse (at least
in its non-revolutionary forms) took account of the observation that, for example, cholera and yellow fever struck
preferentially amongst the poor. The same areas of the city,
namely the dwelling places of misery, nourished sickness and
insurrection. A new police, a *police de santé*, was required,
just as La Mare had written a century before. The optimal
result would be collections of workers' houses that were
relatively large, open, and well aired but that did not
afford too many opportunities for social intercourse.
"There was no architectural solution to the problem of social
contagion: it was necessary to open the worker's domicile
to the outside (air and light) even while shutting him off
from his neighbours. It was necessary to increase the light
while decreasing visibility. It was necessary to create a
space where currents of air criss-crossed but never workers.
The city must be both open and closed."[200] The assumption,
obviously, was that workers' *habitus* would be changed by
improving their habitat. But workers were dangerous even if
they were well fed: what was threatening was their getting
together, whether their stomachs were full or empty. So
the question of control still remained. The architectural
answer, small houses grouped around large factories, the
Owenite answer, one might say, foundered as a general
solution because people didn't like living next to
factories. "The worker's habitat must square a circle:
it must separate classes, but it is utopian to wish to
unite them; hygiene demands that workers be given large

lodgings at low prices, but the laws of profit oppose this;
the economy demands a certain degree of collectivization,
but philanthropic politics rejects this. The moralization
of the worker implies that he be given a taste for his own
property, but without it conferring security."[201]   The
answer, clearly, was not architectural but social, the
provision of comfort, a soft discipline that tied the poor
into the economy by giving them something (but not too much)
to lose.

A start was made with the domestic distribution of running
water. The benefits were immense: it eliminated the unhealthy
and immoral centres of social intercourse, the public pumps;
it got rid of an obnoxious and dirty class of individuals,
the public water-carriers who, moreover, could no longer serve
as an illegal mail service nor perform unspeakable actions in
hallways and on the landings of tenements. And it provided
comfort and convenience. From running water to cable TV and
home computers, there has been a steady process by which
machinery has invested the internal space of houses with its
services, responding to a need or a desire, to be sure, but
also riveting bodies and gently reorganizing domestic and
extra-domestic life according to its own imperatives. There
has existed, therefore, a double process characterized, on
the one hand, by an increased autonomy for the domestic cell
so that one could tap more easily the available sources of
energy, fluids, messages, and images from outside, but, on
the other, by a growing dependency of the inhabitant of
the apparatus that enabled him to alter his natural environment. Moreover, it involved the destruction of the city as
a public space by increasing privatization. The paradox or
contradiction of increasing domestication was that, as there
was less left outside that was not domesticated, there was
also less left outside that mattered. What resulted inside
was strictly controlled, but once again, by nobody. Or
rather, the nature of the new police function had changed.

The old police were concerned primarily with monitoring
practical activities either by prohibition or tolerance;
the new police have inserted themselves within the technical
apparatus itself so that control and monitoring of inhabitants and the functioning of necessary services have tended
to become one and the same thing. This is why the telephone
company has been the object of strong emotional ambivalence,
an unanticipated and perhaps amusing consequence of La Mare's
seemingly innocuous desire to know Paris as well as his own
home.[202]

    Within the new regime of hygiene and salubrity, hospitals
had a special role. Between 1772 and 1788 over two-hundred
plans and over fifty detailed architectural documents were
drawn up to construct a reformed Hôtel-Dieu in Paris. The
role of the hospital and, thus, its architecture had to
change: with a medicine of isolation and exclusion, hospitals
needed simply to enclose; with a medicine of salubrity, what
was needed was openness for air and circulating waters.
Hospitals must no longer be permitted to concentrate contagion but ought be transformed into "machines to cure."
The function of the hospital was to be given a physical
expression and bodies would be spatially distributed so that
they could be monitored but not be infectious. No longer
would the hospital be an asylum for the poor but the privileged site of medical practice. The debate on the purpose,
location, size, specialization, rules for admission, and
so on was all directed towards the definition of an architecture appropriate to the most efficient production of a
useful medical space. As with the notion of habitat, the
same amalgam of technology and moralism was at work. The
category of "the poor" was refined into more functionally
specific terms: good poor and bad poor, involuntarily
unemployed poor and poor who refused to work. The purpose
of the new analysis was to make the poor useful by putting
them to work for their keep rather than have them be a drain

on the rest of society. Orphans, for example, should
eventually have to repay society for taking care of them
while they were children. Perhaps they could be drafted
into the military or into factories. Second, the entire
body of society and not just the troublesome fringes, should
be healthy. "Health is an imperative: the duty of each
person and the general objective of society," along with
organizing wealth.[203] Just as political economy would
ensure the enrichment of society, once the categories of
poverty and illness had been distinguished, problems of
health and physical well-being were susceptible to a
technical and political solution, a proper policing of
the social body, by means of economic regulations. The
illnesses of the poor became just one element in the general
question of social health.

The moral promotion of social health also meant the
promotion of social control by the technicians of the newly
medicalized urban space. The old notion of a "regime" as
a combination of a rule of life and a form of preventative
medicine gave way to a collective regime for the whole
population, which called for certain limited but necessary
medical supervision, intervention, and control. At the
very least, doctors took it upon themselves to instruct
their fellow citizens in the fundamental rules of hygiene
and health. They had knowledge of science; old wives had
but tales. In this way medicine, as a general technique of
health, even more than as a service to the sick or as an
art of curing, played an increasingly important role in the
administration of society and thus in the machinery of power.
Eventually this eighteenth-century "medico-administrative"
knowledge turned into nineteenth-century "social economic"
knowledge and twentieth-century "social work." "And it
likewise constituted a politico-medical grip on a population that was then enrolled in a whole series of prescrip-
tion dealing not just with illness but with general forms of

existence and behaviour (eating and drinking, sexuality and fecundity, ways of dressing, the kinds of homes people should live in, and so forth)." These developments, obviously, raised the status of doctors. There were more of them, which meant that the job had become attractive, and they found places in academies and institutes, as counsellors to the great, members of learned assemblies and societies, of government and royal commissions. A new social type emerged, the doctor who was also a political and economic reformer. "The doctor became the great adviser and expert if not in the art of governing at least in that of observing, correcting and improving the social 'body' and keeping it in a state of permanent good health."[204] This was the social side of the clinical gaze. Indeed, the creation of hospitals as places where time could be devoted to illness, to the inscription of its characteristics in notebooks and charts and dossiers simultaneously reduced the sick person to an encoded contingency and exalted the doctor as the repository of knowledge. The permanent and obligatory surveillance of sick bodies by the doctor was an experience very close to the scrutiny that God once made of men's sinful souls.

Social work and community mental health provided a final example of a technique for normalization. These new applied sciences were also tied to the rise of medicine as an instrument of social control. The initial change substituted the problem of childhood for the problem of children. That is, instead of being concerned only with numbers of children born and their mortality rates, medicine was concerned also with the organization of a social phase or category, with the conditions under which they survived and the moral and economic investments involved. Innoculation and vaccination extended the medical policing of families into the home. "The medical policies that were outlined in the eighteenth century in all the countries of Europe had their first effect in the organization of the family, or rather, of the

complex family-children, as the first and immediate instance
of the medicalization of individuals; they played the role
of mediator between the general objectives concerning the
good health of the social body and the desire or need for
individual care; this policy allowed for the articulation
of a 'private' ethic of good health (which was a reciprocal
duty for both parents and children) under the collective
rubric of hygiene, and a scientific technique of curing,
which was supported by the requirements of individuals
and families, and furnished by a professional body of
qualified doctors certified by the state."[205] All the
apparatus of nineteenth-century care, the market where
supply of services met demands of the sick, the intervention
of authorities to promote public health, the privileged
relationship of doctor and patient--all that could take
place only on the basis of the earlier formation of the
"medicalized" family. By capturing the market long domin-
ated by the old wives, the young medical men brought the
surveillance of the state into the heart of the family. The
doctor formed an alliance with the mother against the servants
as well as against the father. Patriarchy was undermined at
the same time that the private space of the family was opened,
by the medical spies, to a servicing that was ultimately
supervised and administered by the state.

"Social housing" sought to combine the advantages of
a hovel, that is, a shelter, a "haven in a heartless world,"
with a barracks. The disadvantages of hovels were that they
were unsanitary but also that they were a refuge and a hiding
place, a space of autonomy. The disadvantage of a barracks
was that gigantic aggregations were also invitations to riot.
The ideal was "to organize a space large enough to be
hygenic, small enough so that only the family could live
in it, and distributed in such a way that the parents could
monitor their children."[206] Likewise, social assistance
was intended to overcome the inefficiencies of sheer

repression and the ideological difficulties involved with
charity. When the poor gained political visibility, it became
increasingly difficult simply to suppress their aspirations.
But this made the question of charity more delicate: to make
it a right would contradict liberalism. Thus the alliance of
bourgeois and proletarian against the arbitrary power of the
old regime fell apart: the interests of the proletarians
lay in maintaining the ties between state reorganization
and the provision of public services while that of the
bourgeois lay in dissociating the two. Philanthropy and
"advice" to the poor was always possible but it also presented a danger, in the eyes of the liberal bourgeois, of
turning into charity. What was needed was "legitimate
influence," that is, material assistance as a means to
induce the poor to accept moral advice. It could be made
effective only after an inspection of the poor person's
circumstances. Thus the "means test" tied morality to the
economy and ensured that poor families would be surveyed--
the details of family life must be known if fraud is to be
prevented. In this way the difference with charity was
safely established: charity was based on external criteria
such as religious practice or family respectability; the new
benevolence was organized by means of internal surveillance.

Problems could be anticipated. The home, after all, is
supposed to be inviolable and the parents sovereign over
their offspring. Moral deficiency would have to be defined
legally so as to enable philanthropic notables to intervene
(much like doctors) and override "natural" parental authority.
In the name of defending women and children, philanthropical
spies could scrutinize families to see if crimes were
committed *by* children (in which case they would mediate the
family and the judiciary) or *against* children (in which case
they were their first defence). In principle, that is,
philanthropists and their present-day successors enticed
moral order by embodying the threat of more strenuous

activity. In order to avoid oppression (which might turn
into open resistance), a complex tutelary structure, with
social workers at the strategic junction of family, judiciary,
psychiatry, and education, have been established to promote
the supervised development of "difficult" children (or
families). If supervision of irregularity does not work,
the family can be destroyed and its members enrolled in the
order of delinquents.[207]

In order to harmonize family authority and "normal"
socialization, the consumption of meaning and symbols must
be carefully controlled and administered--by psychologists
and social workers, of course, but also by advertising,
schools, newspapers and so on. That is, the discourse that
governs the images of family life both expressed the problem
of family disintegration and provided the solution to it.
Again there was a perfect conjunction of power-knowledge,
created just in time, as it were, to prevent families from
flying apart or collapsing into themselves. Social workers
and allied agents claimed neutrality with respect to family
conflicts and family difficulties; this gave them the ability
to manage contradictions. The technique consisted in regu-
lating images. What escaped the technique was everything
that was aleatory in bodily being, everything that involved
the harmonizing of bodies, everything that expressed the
desire to live. All these things were seen by the "psy-
technicians" as rebellion, which indeed they were.

The intended result of the provision of comfort and
convenience of habitat, of creating machines to cure, of
providing the philanthropical policing of families was to
ensure that normality be maintained and abnormality be
corrected. The category of the abnormal was also born in
the nineteenth century alongside the institutions of supervision, control, surveillance and classification that have
been discussed already. Three elements went into the
formation of the category of the abnormal. The most ancient

was the human monster. The monster violated both judicial
and natural laws: he did not conform to the frame of the
species and he committed forbidden acts. His ambiguous
status is still present in abnormality: it may be an
exception within nature or it may be a legal infraction.
From a "monstrous" act, like that of Pierre Rivière, it was
a short step to a "dangerous" individual who, nevertheless,
could be given neither a medical definition nor a judicial
status, but who constituted "the fundamental notion of
contemporary expertise."[208]   A second constituent was the
"incorrigible." Not an illegal person nor a violation of
nature, this more recent personality violated the imperatives of training. He did not respond properly to the
new disciplinary techniques of the army, the school, the
factory, the family. Special institutions have had to be
created to deal with those who could not be trained in the
ordinary way. These include, besides the rebellious, the
blind, deaf, dumb, imbecilic, retarded, nervous and unstable.
And lastly, the onanist, an eighteenth-century novelty, made
his special contribution to abnormality. By adding onanism
to the traditionally prohibited acts of adultery, incest,
sodomy, and bestiality, the ultimate *dispositif* was set
into position in order to control the smaller movements of
concupiscence. Since the movement against masturbation
was directed first against the infants and children of the
leisured and idle rich, it was not simply a technique to
repress proletarian pleasure in the service of greater
productivity. What it did was place sexuality at the
centre of a host of bodily illnesses, especially the
"illness" that might emerge (perhaps years later) as a
consequence of the sexual use of one's own body. And, if
a child was guilty of "abuse" in this way, his parents were
equally to blame for having failed to supervise him properly.
It could lead to his later seduction by debauched servants
or wicked teachers. "The crusade against masturbation

effected the preparation of the nuclear family (parents and
children) as the mechanism of power-knowledge. The introduction of the question of infant sexuality and all the
anomalies for which it would be responsible was one of the
procedures by which this new apparatus was constituted. The
small incestuous family that characterizes our societies,
the miniscule and sexually saturated family space that we
were raised in and where we live was formed there."[209]
All three, the monster, the incorrigible and the onanist,
came together in the theory of degeneracy, which served as
the framework of knowledge within which the techniques of
adjustment, classification and intervention were carried
out.[210] It led to the creation of an institutional complex
within medicine and law that both took care of abnormals and
defended society. And most importantly, it led to the
elevation of the most recent constituent, infantile sexuality,
into the main explanatory factor of all abnormalities and
the principle of interpretation. This was the topic of
Foucault's most recent work.

SEXUALITY: THE ULTIMATE DISPOSITIF

11

Foucault's latest project is a multivolume history of
sexuality. As with his earlier work, he emphasized the heterogeneity of human reality and the contemporary conjunction of
power and knowledge that has tended to obscure it. On the
one side there is the application of power that has resulted
in the history of exclusion, the exclusion of the mad, the
poor, the sick, the proletarian, the delinquent. In addition,
however, he has brought that familiar history into contact
with a more obscure and embarrassing history of delimitations
based upon sexuality, sexuality that is normal or perverted,
male or female, adult or infantile.[211] Exclusion had nothing
to do with sexuality until the nineteenth century; then the
technology of sexuality was woven together with the technology that excluded madness. The negative power of exclusion
was thereby rendered positive; the initial binary divisions
have grown more complex and the result is a grand technology
of the psyche "that makes sex at once the hidden truth of
reasonable consciousness and the decipherable meaning of
madness: their common meaning thus allows for the manipu-
lation of both by means of the same modalities."[212] Sexuality is not, therefore, sex. It is not a biological means
for reproduction of the species, not something that gives
pleasure, not the body and interpersonal relations. These
heterogeneous elements are brought together by the *dispositif*
of sexuality that arranged them all in a line and gave the
whole its proper functioning. Sexuality, in short, is the
mediator between power and sex, the means of harnessing
human energies and human pleasures for the production of
truth. Thus, sexuality operates by way of an economy of

the body and pleasure, or rather, of the scarcity of
pleasure and/or the illegitimacy of pleasure. Once we
know that all pleasure is secretly sexual, that knowledge
can be invoked as the justification for the application of
power in service of moderation and control.

The contemporary status of sexuality was a bourgeois
achievement of a piece with its other posthistorical
activities, consumerism, public health, contraception, racism,
jogging, and so forth. All of these things presuppose, as
was mentioned earlier, the exaltation of the transient body
over the previously eternal soul, the replacement of sin by
sickness. The historical origins, however, lay in the tight
little Christian dialectic of the flesh. On the positive
side, because the word was made flesh and dwelt among us,
salvation may be granted to the faithful; but on the negative
side, the sins of the flesh will surely bring damnation. And
with a minimum of interpretation the world of the flesh could
be transfigured into the world simply. But then again,
expiation was possible. In the judicial order, the marks
of penance may be directly inscribed by inflicting pain.
In the religious order, the spirit may gain absolution
through confession. And it was confession, not torture,
that had been transmitted from the old regime into the eroti-
cized discourse of the present world. Confession was
reciprocal: it bound the confessor and the penitent
together in a relationship of mutual dependence; there
was a complicity of the confessor in the sins (and pleasures)
of the sinner.[213] Confession, therefore, was a means to make
visible what had been repressed, which suggested once again
the reciprocity between prohibition and expression. One may
say, in effect, that the pleasures of confession were simply
discursive recapitulations of the pleasures of non-discursive
practice that they made articulate.

In any event, it was into this double world that Foucault
plunged. "My aim is to examine the case of a society that has

loudly been castigating itself for its hypocrisy for more
than a century, that speaks verbosely of its own silence,
takes great pains to relate in detail the things it does
not say, denounces the powers it exercises, and promises to
liberate itself from the very laws that have made it
function."[214] That is, Foucault sought to delineate a
regime of power and knowledge, to be sure, but also its
ties to pleasure and the way that that complex sustains the
discourse about sexuality; or again, he wished to explore the
injunction that turned desire into discourse, including that
discourse prohibited by conventions of decency. Indeed, those
conventions constituted the arm by which sexual energies were
administered, were made useful and productive, were policed
and directed towards the creation of truths. A contemporary
teacher, for example, risks losing tenure, at least in some
places, if, as did Erasmus in his *Dialogues*, she offered
advice on the choice of a good doxy. We may talk exhaustively
about it; we may study Erasmus or the sociology and economics
of prostitution, but we do not say much that is practical
about the activity itself. "Whether in the form of a subtle
confession in confidence or an authoritarian interrogation,
sex--be it refined or rustic--had to be put into words."[215]
Moreover, all this subtle talk about silent pleasures
expressed the exercise of power. In no way did it suppress
it. "What is peculiar to modern societies, in fact, is not
that they consigned sex to a shadow existence, but that they
dedicated themselves to speaking of it *ad infinitum*, while
exploiting it as *the* secret."[216] For example, the legal
prohibitions on acts such as sodomy or libertinage were
refined during the nineteenth century. The pervert was
not one who violated the law, who temporarily flouted acceptable behaviour, but one whose very being was abnormal: he
(or she) had a history, a childhood, a *Lebensform*, physiology,
and psychic profile to be uncovered, of course, by examination,
observation and interrogation. Increasingly vigilant speech

brought to light ever more delicate perversions. An array
of strange names, which also demonstrated the inventiveness
of a "sexologist's" command of Latin and Greek, did not
suppress sexuality but, just the opposite, brought it into
visible, analytic clarity. Those peculiar nelogisms at the
same time rendered sexuality exciting and an object of discourse, much as the psychoanalyst's consulting room, with
its couch, resembled the whore's bedroom. Both enabled the
apparatus of repression to function smoothly.

The medicalization of sexual peculiarities presupposed
a technology of health and sickness. Once sexuality was
turned into a medicalizable object it had to be detected
and described--in the depths of the organism, in a smile, in
the colour of one's skin, in the signs of the slightest
behaviour. Moreover, the detection and the pleasures
detected reinforced one another: "an impetus was given to
power through its very exercise; and emotion rewarded the
supervising control and carried it further; the intensity of
the confession renewed the questioner's curiosity; the
pleasure that was discovered fed back to the power that
encircled it."[217] This perpetual spiral of power, discourse
and pleasure had the delightful implication that the society
that undertook its operation was, by definition, perverse.
There were no limits to sexuality; it extended everywhere,
penetrated the tiniest gesture, the least significant act.
"Modern society is perverse, not in spite of its puritanism
or as if from a backlash provoked by its hypocrisy; it is
in actual fact, and directly, perverse."[218] *In actual fact:*
the manifold and fixated sexualities of infant and child,
the relational sexuality of doctor and patient, of teacher
and pupil, the spatial sexualities of home, school, and
prison, were all correlated with power; and *directly:*
through medicine, psychiatry, prostitution, pornography.
All these centres of power, which attend to sexuality and
manifest it in speech, also intensify pleasures and spread

them further, thus ensuring further analysis, further discourse, further speech. In a word, if modern society were
not actually and directly perverse it would not seek, in
discursive practice, the truth of its own perversity. And
it does, constantly. Thus does one encounter the same
devious amalgam of technology and moralism. Scientific
language does not speak of sex itself but of aberrations,
perversions, and oddities. Its purpose is not medical
description but the use of medical norms to express fears
and uphold a morality. And, as with similar discourses
discussed earlier, its evasions were all the more effective
for being indirect.

If, then, one may say that medical theories of sexuality
expressed a kind of will to nonknowledge, to moralism and its
pleasures, it is also true that it was fully balanced by a
will to knowledge that was, in part at least, expressed by
the physiology of reproduction, by sex. Two complimentary
procedures enacted two distinct but complementary, that is
dialectically related, hermeneutic canons. The first procedure, which enacts a hermeneutic of reminiscence is *ars
erotica*. Here the truth of sex is drawn from pleasure
itself and is understood as an accumulation of experience,
which is related only to itself, not to any external norm,
and results in a secret knowledge that can be known only in
the mode of participation and transmitted only by a master
to an apprentice. It must be secret, or at least the
ultimate truth must remain incapable of discursive dis-
closure not for reasons of infamy but because partici-
patory revelation is impossible, because revelation extern-
alizes what can be known only from within, and if external-
ized is rendered ineffective. Secondly, however, is *scientia
sexualis*, where the truth of sex is geared to the discursive
power-knowledge of a confession, where what is known is
gained through rigorous demystification.[219]

The contemporary truth of sex is scientific. "For us

it is in the confession that truth and sex are joined, through
the obligatory and exhaustive expression of an individual
secret."[220] The obligation to conceal is more than the pre-
condition for the existence of a duty to admit. Power is
always explicitly involved: one must confess to an authority. There is always modification of the one who confesses
as a result: the person who has confessed is redeemed or
purified by having overcome the obstacles and resistances
that stood in the way of its formulation and that by doing
so confirmed the result, namely purification. If nothing
were there to be overcome, if one did not have an obligation
to speak, there would be no more to the confessional ritual
than conversation. In this regard, it was the great achievement of nineteenth-century society to put into operation
machinery designed to produce the uniform truth of sex,
which also had the consequence of making it an object of
great suspicion. Once again, that is, the mastery that
discourse was intended to grant was less than complete.[221]
Once again, by saying one thing discourse concealed something else, by expressing one power it also called up
resistance to it.

Because sexuality is "an especially dense transfer-
point for power-relations--between men and women, young and
old, parents and children, teachers and pupils, priests and
laity, administration and population," it is "endowed with
the greatest instrumentality, is useful for the greatest
number of maneuvers, and is capable of serving as a point
of support, as a linchpin, for the most varied strategies."[222]
The four great postenlightenment strategies of power-
knowledge centred first upon the hystericization of women's
bodies.[223] Women were declared to be thoroughly sexual,
nervous, and pathological; as part of a social and political strategy they were producers of future citizens. Second
was the pedagogization of children's sex; sexual activity
in children (especially masturbation) became both natural

and contrary to nature so they must be controlled by parents,
doctors, and the vast army of psychologists and social
workers. Third was the socialization of fertility: couples
should be "responsible," which could mean either being for
or against birth control. And last was the psychiatrization
of perverse pleasure with its inevitable accompaniment, the
creation of a corrective technology. These strategies have
produced four powerful images: the hysterical woman, the
masturbating child, the Malthusian couple, and the perverse
adult. When the centre of sexuality, namely the family, went
awry (because of real or virtual incest, masturbation, wife-
neglect or perversion) then it broadcast the long complaint
of its suffering to the experts, the doctors, educators,
psychologists, and priests, who listed and devised technologies of adjustment. But none of this expertise and not
even that of psychoanalysis, whatever its other virtues,
challenged the requirement of confession nor escaped the
dispositif of sexuality. Consequently they could not make
sexuality itself a topic of analysis.

Sexuality, then, led to knowledge and discipline of
the individual body and to the regulation of populations.
It gave access to both the life of the individual and the
life of the species. Accordingly, the nineteenth-century
search for sexuality in its smallest details--in behaviour,
in dreams, in all sorts of madness and folly, in the memories
of a no longer innocent childhood--was a means to gain access
through analysis, which was also the power of mastery. The
importance of the four great strategies, then, was that they
combined discipline with regulation. With the first two,
regularization led to discipline: sexualization of children
and hystericization of women could be justified in terms of
the health of future generations. With the second two,
discipline led to regularization: birth control and perversion could be suppressed in order that things be normal.

There was, finally, a nondiscursive set of results.

First and most obviously, there was yet another confinement.
In the seventeenth century sex was publicly acknowledged.
Then it was shut away, into the home, the conjugal family,
the function of reproduction, the parents' bedroom (where,
nevertheless, it was regulated by the medical gaze of the
state) or into brothels (where the direct arm of the police
maintained a watch on things). The result, however, was a
peculiar sort of misery. No doubt sex has always been a
source of unease and mystery, but contemporary sexuality
allows for an objectless profanation, an empty profanation
of itself. It is a profanation because sex does involve
one in a mysterious participation; it is empty because nothing
is sacred. But this same emptiness, this denial of the limit
of limitlessness, this affirmation of the death of God, is
also an experience of a kind of ecstasy that is not sheer
misery but, just the opposite, is eroticism. "A deed god
and sodomy" said Foucault, in one of his more outrageous
aphorisms, "are the thresholds of the new metaphysical
ellipse."[224] A dead god, for that is the contemporary
inheritance of history and its end; sodomy because nature
provides no guide and sex must have the jolt of a recol-
lection of pleasure; an ellipse, because metaphysics is
never a perfect circle but is always shrunk or stretched.

CONCLUSION: TRUTH AND POWER

12

Foucault has rightly been compared to Freud.[225]   In
the same way that Freud discovered and explored the *terra
incognita* of sexuality, Foucault, following Nietzsche has
identified and toured the unspoken realm of power.
Before Freud sexuality was reduced to sex; by considering
power as productive materiality, as any kind of technology,
as a Siamese twin of knowledge, and not solely as the
armature of the state or a metaphor for all kinds of human
activity, has Foucault not achieved something similar?   The
state remains the plexus of the finer technologies and the
place at which strategies come to fruition.   The lives of
most people, however, are ordered by other means, by successful socialization, by unnamed fears, by affections.
This is hardly news.   What Foucault discovered was that
these transparent relations, strategies and techniques of
power, which traverse us and help make us what we are, were
accompanied by specific formations and configurations of
knowledge that permitted and produced evident, necessary,
and "natural" truth,   and **did** so   in   such   a   way   that
the power involved disappeared into invisibility.   Inver-
sely, the analysis of knowledge, of discursive practices
and formations, brought to light its function within a
strategy of power that, in any given society, penetrated
and controlled bodies and wills.   From his earliest to
his most recent work, Foucault's meticulous concern for
the great heterogeneity of human life has made visible
the reductive and homogenizing distortions of power-
knowledge.   In *Madness and Civilization* we saw what the
men of reason said about the unreasonable.   And we know

what they did: they locked them up and half a dialogue was
lost.   Power was forcibly joined to truth and the unreasonable were stifled.   In the *History of Sexuality*, power-
knowledge appeared in the form of a double movement: the
sexualization of the body and its desires and pleasures
coupled to a will to produce the truth of this sexualization.
Under the first aspect were the recipes for unhappiness that
we know all too well, the hystericization of women's bodies,
pedagogization of the sex of the child, socialization of
procreative conduct, psychiatrization of perverse pleasures.
Under the second was the force of will and confession that
made truth primarily the truth of sexuality.   And in the
other, more directly "practical" technologies of medicine,
penology, jurisprudence, public health, social science, and
pedagogy, the new knowledge has led to new confinements,
new categories, new restrictions and enclosures.   The
political end has come with the several totalitarianisms of
our age, the great administrative systems for producing death
that have all been justified by one kind of knowledge, truth,
and science, or another.   These things, Foucault insisted,
are not unfortunate errors but "the consequences of the most
'true' theories in the order of politics."[226]

Truth has been given a new meaning.   It is neither outside power nor without power.   The truth is of this world;
it is produced there thanks to numerous constraints.   And
there it serves to regulate the effects of power.   Every
society has its regime of truth, its general politics of
truth, that serves to regulate the production, distribution, functioning and circulation of some discourses
and not of others.   It is emphatically not an ideological
superstructure behind which lies the "real" truth, pristine,
unsullied, supercelestial, and disclosed by a subtle knowledge.   In our present posthistorical and technological
societies, "the 'political economy' of truth is characterized by five historically important attributes: 'truth'

is centred on the form of scientific discourse and on the institutions that produce it; it is subjected to constant economic and political instigation (there is a need for truth in political and economic production); it is the object, in several different forms, of an immense distribution and consumption (it circulates in educational or informational apparatuses that extend widely, though in a strictly limited way, throughout the social body); it is produced and transmitted under the dominant but not exclusive control of great political or economic machines (universities, the army, writing, the media); lastly, it constitutes the entire stakes of political debate and social confrontation ('ideological' struggles)."[227] When truth has become a weapon by which society manages itself, the task of thinkers (or philosophers or, if you like, of intellectuals) has been changed.

By a long tradition, the philosopher is supposed to be "on the side" of truth or "in favour" of truth. That dream has been all dreamed out. With the end of history and the end of that picture gallery of representations and powers that Hegel chronicled and accounted for, with the advent, that is, of the present world that we inherited long before we (or Foucault) were born, the purpose of thought has become the discovery of the status of truth and the political and economic role it plays. One thinks today by undertaking that discursive practice that accounts for the way that truth is geared to the restraints of scarcity but also to the exuberance of recognition, that accounts for the way that truth is able to justify the invisibility of those it eclipses but also the glory of those it exalts. In a large measure this means no more than expressing what is common knowledge. But one must do so by unblocking what a subtle system of power-knowledge has invalidated by rendering too familiar. The special problem for thinkers, for those few genuine historians of the present, is that they may be part of this

power system either as outright apologists or, more honour-
ably, in virtue of their role as a "conscience to power."
To accept the role of conscience is to be a jester. To
avoid playing the fool one must undertake a more difficult
and more serious (though not necessarily more sombre) struggle
against the power that transforms one's discourse into an
object that can be indexed with the tag "conscience of
society." Truth telling has again become a pragmatic
political activity. The actual conduct of a contemporary
truth teller will, of course, vary according to one's
opportunity, disposition, courage, intelligence, imagination,
and so on. The grey limits and colourful opportunities are
both set, it seems to me, by the following analogy of
circumstance. In the early Christian centuries men wondered
about the return of Christ and what to do in the meantime.
Nowadays the second coming seems to be that of revolution.
And yet, so many have been betrayed. The messages of the
modern synoptic gospellers has been seared into our being
even as we await the transfigurative discourse of a contemporary St. John, whom we shrewdly suspect cannot exist.

NOTES

[1] "Foucault répond à Sartre," *La Quinzaine littéraire*, (1 mars 1969), 21.

[2] See Foucault, "Jean Hyppolite (1907-1968)," *Revue de métaphysique et de morale* 74 (1969), 131-6, and "The Discourse on Language" tr. Rupert Swyer, in *The Archeology of Knowledge*, Tr. A. M. Sheridan Smith (New York, Harper, 1972), 235 ff. See also Alan Sheridan, *Michel Foucault: The Will to Truth*, (London, Tavistock, 1980), 2-5.

[3] Foucault, "Débat sur le roman," *Tel Quel*, 17 (1964), 14. See also "The Discourse of Language," *passim*, and "Theatrum Philosophicum" in *Language, Counter-Memory, Practice: Selected Essays and Interviews*, ed., D. F. Bouchard, tr., D. F. Bouchard and S. Simon, (Ithaca, Cornell University Press, 1977), 184-6. Kojève's argument concerning the Sage or Wise Man is set out in *Introduction à la Lecture de Hegel*, 2nd ed. (Paris, Gallimard, 1947), 271 ff.

[4] "Entretien" in Raymond Bellour, *Le Livre des autres*, (Paris, Herne, 1971), 141.

[5] "Foucault répond à Sartre," *La Quinzaine litteraire*, (1 mars, 1969), 20.

[6] "Entretien," *Arts et loisirs*, 38 (15 juin, 1966), 9.

[7] "Entretien: la publication des *Oeuvres complètes de Nietzsche*," *Le Monde*, (24 mai, 1967), viii.

[8] "Entretien" in Bellour, *op. cit.*, 204.

[9] *Ibid.*, 144.

[10] "La folie n'existe que dans une société," *Le Monde*, (27 juillet, 1961), 9.

[11] *Mental Illness and Psychology*, tr. Alan Sheridan, (New York, Harper, 1976), 10.

[12]*Mental Illness and Psychology*, 63, 87–8, 73.

[13]"Introduction" to Binswanger, *Le Rêve et l'existence*, (Bruges, Desclée de Brouwer, 1954), 111.

[14]*Ibid.*, 49.

[15]*Ibid.*, 85.

[16]*Ibid.*, 127.

[17]*Le Cycle de la structure*, trans. Foucault and Daniel Rocher, (Bruges, Desclée de Brouwer, 1958).

[18]*Folie et déraison: Histoire de la folie à l'âge classique*, (Paris, Plon, 1961), viii. This preface was replaced in the enlarged edition (Paris, Gallimard, 1972). References are given where possible to the shortened (and sometimes slightly altered) English translation by R. Howard, *Madness and Civilization: A History of Insanity in the Age of Reason*, (New York, Pantheon, 1965).

[19]The reaction of French psychiatrists was uniformly hostile. See *Evolution psychiatrique*, 36 (1971), 222–298, for a series of lengthy and angry denunciations.

[20]*Mental Illness and Psychology*, 60.

[21]*Folie et déraison*, v. See also *Mental Illness and Psychology*, 76.

[22]*La Folie et la chose littéraire*, (Paris, Seuil, 1978), 349.

[23]See Roland Barthes, "Savoir et folie," *Critique*, 174, (1961), 921–22.

[24]*Madness and Civilization*, 11.

[25]*Madness and Civilization*, 16.

[26]*Madness and Civilization*, 35.

[27]*Madness and Civilization*, 57.

[28]A central text in this respect (to be discussed further below) is Nicolas de la Mare, *Traité de la Police*, 4 vols. (Paris, Michel Brunet, 1722-1738), begun under Louis XIV. Police functions are repeated, practically unchanged in Hegel's *Philosophy of Right*, which suggests an important difference between the theory of the (police) state, as articulated by continental thinkers, and the theory of government, which prevails in Anglo-American political thought.

[29]See the discussion between Michel Foucault and David Cooper, "Enferment, Psychiatrie, Prison," *Change*, 32-3 (1977), 76-110. The topic of "social danger" is dealt with below.

[30]*Madness and Civilization*, 146.

[31]One imagines the rational cogito *saying* this. One also imagines that secretly it was saying "I think, therefore I am not mad (I think)."

[32]Foucault, "Resumé du cours, 1974-1975," Collège de France, *Annuaire*, (Paris, Imprimerie Palais Royal, 1975), 293.

[33]*Ibid.*, 294.

[34]*Loc. cit.*

[35]*Ibid.*, 298. For more details, see Robert Castel, *L'Ordre psychiatrique: l'âge d'or de l'aliénisme*, (Paris, Minuit, 1976). An account of parallel developments in England is in Andrew T. Scull, "From Madness to Mental Illness: Medical men as moral Entrepreneurs," *Archives européens de sociologie*, 16 (1975), 218-61.

[36]Foucault, "Résumé du cours, 1974-1975," 299.

[37]Foucault, "L'Asile illimité" *Le Nouvel Observateur*, 646 (28 mars, 1977), 67.

[38]See also Jacques Donzelot, "Espace close: travail et moralisation," *Topique*, 3 (mai, 1970), 125-52.

[39] "Résumé du cours, 1974–1975," 296–7.   See also the extensive discussion of drug therapy, lobotomy, hypothalmic excisions, etc., in Henri Dougier, ed., "Guérir pour normaliser," *Autrement*, 4 (1975–6) and especially Jean-Pierre Peter, "Le grand rêve de l'ordre médical, en 1770 et aujourd' hui," *Autrement*, 4 (1975–6), 183–92.

[40] *Madness and civilization*, 222.

[41] Foucault, "Enferment, Psychiatrie, Prison," 95.

[42] "Résumé du cours, 1974–1975," 300.

[43] "Each culture, after all, gets the madness it deserves. And if Artaud is mad and if the psychiatrists are allowed to confine him, that is already quite a picture and the finest possible eulogy--for the psychiatrists."   Foucault, "Entretien," *Le Monde*, (22 juillet, 1961).   Hans Jonas reported that magnificent opinion of a geneticist, that the technology of amniocentesis has finally made it possible for "mankind" to avoid the "price" of epilepsy.   If that meant that a Dostoevsky would be aborted, fine.   "Mankind, she said, cannot afford that price for genius and should wait for a Dostoevsky without epilepsy." *Philosophical Essays: From Ancient Creed to Technological Man*, (Englewood Cliffs, Prentice-Hall 1974), 151 fn. 10.

[44] *Madness and Civilization*, 228.

[45] "Entretien: la folie n'existe que dans une société," *Le Monde* (27 juillet, 1961), 9.

[46] "Débat sur le roman," *Tel Quel*, 17 (1964), 45.

[47] In addition to *Raymond Roussel* (Paris, Gallimard, 1963), Foucault wrote a study of Reveroni de St-Cyr, a nineteenth-century eroticist and soldier, "Un si cruel savoir," *Critique*, 182 (1962), 597–611, translated Leo Spitzer, *Etudes de style* (Paris, Gallimard, 1962), and wrote essays on Bataille, "Preface à la transgression," *Critique*, 195–196 (1963) 761–9, on Roger Laporte, "Guetter le jour qui vient" *NRF*, 130 (oct., 1963), 709–16, on the "new novel," "Distance aspect, origine," *Critique* 198 (1963), 931–45, on Pierre Klossowski, "La prose d'Actéon," *NRF* 135 (1964), 444–59 as well as on Mallarmé, Nerval, Rousseau, Jules Verne, Maurice Blanchot and Flaubert.   In addition, Foucault wrote several essays on language.   For a brief discussion of all this, see Raymond Bellour, "L'Homme, les mots," *Magazine Littéraire*, 101 (juin, 1975), 19–23.

[48] *Raymond Roussel*, 40.

[49] *Ibid.*, 99-100.

[50] *Ibid.*, 155-6.

[51] *Ibid.*, 109-10. Foucault also undertook a brief study of another writer who also had a peculiar view of language, Jean-Pierre Brisset, "7 propos sur le 7e ange," preface to Brisset, *La Grammaire Logique, suivi de la science de dieu*, (Paris, Tchou, 1970). Brisset, who also wrote *Le Mystère de Dieu est accompli*, held that words were essentially sounds, not thoughts, so he undertook what amounts to a series of word-games (e.g., salaud, sale eau, salle aux pris, salle aux pris (onnières), saloperie, which means: son-of-a-bitch, dirty water, expensive room, prisoners' room, filth). Apropos of Foucault's shaven head and fondness for turtleneck sweaters. One could imagine a similar series: tortue, tortu, tortues, torteux, torture and perhaps even tort and tortil.

[52] *The Birth of the Clinic: An Archeology of Medical Perception*, tr., A. M. Sheridan Smith, (New York Vintage, 1975), ix. It was originally published in 1963.

[53] *The Birth of the Clinic*, xi. See also *Folie et déraison*, ii.

[54] *The Birth of the Clinic*, xviii.

[55] Foucault, "Entrevue: le jeu de Michel Foucault," *Ornicar?* 10 (1977), 77-8.

[56] "For *The Birth of the Clinic* I read, for the period 1780-1820, every medical work that had any methodological importance. There are no choices to be made and none can exist. One must read everything and study everything. In other words, one must have available the general archive of an era at a given moment. And in the strict sense, archeology is the science of this archive." "Entretien avec Michel Foucault," in Bellour, *Le livre des autres*, 139.

[57] *The Birth of the Clinic*, 17.

[58] *Ibid.*, 23, 25.

[59]Jacques Donzelot, "Le Troisième âge de la répression," *Topique*, 6 (1971), 97.

[60]*The Birth of the Clinic*, 38. See also Jean-Pierre Peter, "Les Mots et les objets de la maladie," *Revue historique*, 246 (1971), 13-38.

[61]*Ibid.*, 84.

[62]*Ibid.*, 85.

[63]*Ibid.*, 105.

[64]*Ibid.*, 109.

[65]*Ibid.*, 115. See also Jean-Pierre Peter, "Le Corps du delit," *Nouvelle revue de psychanalyse*, 3 (1971), 71-108.

[66]*Ibid.*, 138.

[67]*Ibid.*, 141.

[68]*Ibid.*, 144.

[69]*Ibid.*, 155.

[70]*Ibid.*, 163.

[71]*Ibid.*, 196.

[72]Of the secondary material I have read, only Angèle Kremer-Marietti, *Foucault et l'archeologie du savoir*, (Paris, Seghers, 1974), 180 ff, has paid much attention to the place of this study. The more audacious work seems to have had a wider appeal.

[73]*The Birth of the Clinic*, 197.

[74]*L'Archeologie du savoir*, (Paris, Gallimard, 1969); Tr. A. M. Sheridan Smith, *The Archeology of Knowledge*, (New York, Harper, 1976); *Les Mots et les choses*, (Paris, Gallimard, 1966); tr. Anon., *The Order of Things: An Archeology of the Human Sciences*, (London, Tavistock, 1970).

[75]In this respect see also Foucault "Résponse à une question," *Esprit* N.S. 371 (1968), 850-74.

[76]*The Order Of Things*, xxii, 275; see also *Archeology of Knowledge*, 191.

[77]*The Order Of Things*, 168. As Georges Canguilhem wrote, "the *Episteme*, for any given culture, is in some way the universal system of reference for the age; the only relation it has to its successor is one of difference." "Mort de l'homme ou epuisement du cogito?" *Critique*, 242 (1967), 611. See also Michel Amoit, "Le Relativisme culturaliste de Michel Foucault," *Les Temps modernes*, 248 (1967) 1271-98, and Serge Valdinoci, "Les incertitudes de l'Archéologie: Arché et Archive," *Revue de Métaphysique et de Morale*. 83 (1978), 73-101.

[78]*Ibid.*, 200.

[79]See *Archeology of Knowledge*, 135 ff., 164 f.

[80]*The Order Of Things*, 207. See also Gilles Deleuze, "L'Homme, une existence douteuse," *Le Nouvel Observateur*, 81 (1 juin, 1966), 32-4.

[81]*The Order Of Things*, 226.

[82]*Ibid.*, 228.

[83]*Ibid.*, 229.

[84]*Ibid.*, 73.

[85]*Ibid.*, 244.

[86]There was obviously, a Kantian as well as a Nietzschean resonance to Foucault's own "philosophy." As Jean Lacroix pointed out, the episteme, as a condition of knowledge and an historical *apriori*, certainly had a Kantian flavour. "Fin d'humanisme," *Le Monde*, (juin 9, 1966), 13. See also Mikel Dufrenne, *Pour l'homme*, (Paris, Sevil, 1968), Ch. 3.

[87]*The Order Of Things*, 245.

[88]*Ibid.*, 257.

[89]*Loc. cit.*

[90]*Ibid.*, 259.

[91]*Ibid.*, 260.

[92]*Ibid.*, 261.

[93]*Ibid.*, 262

[94]*Ibid.*, 262-3.

[95]*Ibid.*, 263.

[96]*Ibid.*, 278.

[97]*Loc. cit.*

[98]*Ibid.*, 285.

[99]*Ibid.*, 298.

[100]*Ibid.*, 300.

[101]*Ibid.*, 313.

[102]*Ibid.*, 317.

[103]*Ibid.*, 317.

[104]*Ibid.*, 318.

[105]*Ibid.* The "end of man" is clearly the most outrageous of Foucault's aphorisms. The oceans of ink spilled on the topic betray the outrages of humanism. To say the least, such anger is misplaced: the other side of the horizon of the end of history is precisely the space for thought that is needed to come to terms with modernity.

[106]*Ibid.*, 331.

[107]*Ibid.*, 357.

[108]*Ibid.*, 328.

[109]As Foucault himself explained: "Rather than seek to explain this *savoir* from the point of view of the practico-inert, I am looking to formulate an anlysis from what might be called the 'theoretico-active.'" "Entretien," in R. Bellour, *Le Livre des autres*, 138.

[110]*Ibid.*, 387.

[111]*Ibid.*, 342.

[112]*Archeology of Knowledge*, 205, 210-11.

[113]"Entretien: le jeu de Michel Foucault" *Ornicar?* 10 (1977), 75.

[114]*The Archeology of Knowledge*, 105.

[115]*Ibid.*, 209-10.

[116]For what it is worth, the chief memory I have from 1968-69, which I spent in Paris, was the sense of fun found among the *enragés* and the deep solemnity of their elders, at which it was difficult not to suppress a smirk. One can still sense this in a film such as "Jonah who will be twenty-five in the year 2000." Almost everything I have read that has been written about May '68 and its aftermath talked about politics and revolution, as if it were another Kronstadt. But then the men of 1917 thought they were re-doing 1789, and *they* thought they were Romans.

[117]"Nietzsche, Genealogy, History," in *Language Counter-Memory, Practice*, 139-64.

[118]"Entretien sur la prison: le livre et sa methode," *Magazine littéraire* , 101 (juin, 1975), 33.

[119]"Nietzsche, Genealogy, History," 162-3.

[120]Translated by Rupert Swyer as *The Discourse on Language* and printed as an appendix to *The Archeology of Knowledge*, 215-37.

[121] *The Discourse on Language*, 216.

[122] *Michel Foucault: The Will to Truth*, 130.

[123] "Résumé du cours et traveaux" College de France, *Annuaire*, (Paris, Presses du Palais Royal, 1971), 245.

[124] "Entretien: Le jeu de Michel Foucault," *Ornicar?* 10 (1977), 63-4.

[125] Michel Foucault, ed., *Moi, Pierre Rivière, ayant égorgé ma mère, ma soeur, et mon frère . . .: Un cas de parricide au xixe siècle*, (Paris, Gallimard-Julliard, 1973). In 1975 René Allio made a movie based on the text. Foucault made a cameo appearance--as a judge. See *Le Nouvel Observateur*, 624 (25 oct., 1976), 18.

[126] Philippe Riot, "Les vies paralleles de Pièrre Riviere," in Foucault, ed., *Moi, Pierre Rivière*, 300.

[127] Robert Castel, "Les Médicins et les juges," in Foucault, ed., *op. cit.*, 329.

[128] The assimilation of regicide to parricide was a touchy political issue. There was to be an attempt against Louis Philippe, whose father was considered a regicide, in 1835. The context for the assimilation of the terms was that the family was a mini-society, an organized hierarchy. See Blandine Barret-Kriegel, "Regicide-parricide," in Foucault, ed., *op. cit.*, 285-91.

[129] *Moi, Pierre Rivière*, 128-9.

[130] See Jean-Pierre Peter "Ogres d'archives," *Nouvelle revue de psychanalyse*, 6 (1972), 249-67, for a discussion of several early nineteenth-century discourses on cannibalism and their relation to the "Corsican ogre" who "was but the paradigm of all the others but who managed to gain the summit of worldly success in this matter."

[131] Thus he wrote (p. 137): "Je meurs pour lui [his father] rendre la paix et la tranquilité."

[132]Consider the remarks of Jean-Pierre Peter and Jeanne
Favret, "L,Animal, le fou, la mort," in Foucault, ed., *op. cit.*,
243-64.

[133]Michel Foucault, "Les Meutres qu'on raconte" in
Foucault, ed., *op. cit.*, 271.

[134]Foucault, "Les Meurtres qu'on raconte." 274. Under
the law of 1838, which is still basically in force in France,
people can be committed *before* doing anything criminal if
they are certified mad. In this respect it has become a
worthy successor to the *lettre de cachet de famille* discussed earlier.

[135]"Résumé du cours," Collège de France, *Annuaire*
(Paris, Presses du Palais Royal, 1972), 283.

[136]*Ibid.*, 285.

[137]*Discipline and Punish: The Birth of the Prison*,
tr., Alan Sheridan, (New York, Pantheon, 1977).

[138]Michelle Perrot, ed., *L'Impossible prison: recherches
sur le système pénétentiare au xix*e *siècle, débat avec Michel
Foucault,* (Paris, Seuil, 1980), 44.

[139]Foucault, "Entretien sur la prison: le livre et sa
méthode," *Magazine littéraire*, 101 (juin, 1975), 27.

[140]This list of "reforms" could serve as chapter
headings for works such as N. H. Julius, *Lecons sur les
prisons*, 2 vols., (Paris, Levrault, 1831).

[141]See Jacques Donzelot, "Espace clos: travail et
moralisation," *Topique*, 3 (1970), 125-52, and *idem.*,
"Le troisième age de répression," *Topique*, 6 (1971), 93-130.
See also the following section below.

[142]"Resume du cours," 262.

[143]*Ibid.*, 263.

[144]For further details, see *Discipline and Punish*,
141-61. See also the brilliant study by Georges Vigarello,
Le Corps redressé: Histoire d'un pouvoir pédagogique,
(Paris, Delarge, 1978).

[145]"Résumé du cours," 266.

[146]Foucault, "Entretien: Des supplices aux cellues,"
Le Monde, (21 fév. 1975), 16.

[147]The most famous example is, of course, Jeremy
Bentham's *Panopticon*, whose title page carried the advice:
"Panopticon; or, the Inspection-House: containing the idea
of a new principle of construction applicable to any sort
of establishment, in which persons of any description are
to be kept under inspection; and in particular to peniten-
tiary-houses, prisons, houses of industry, work-houses,
poor-houses, manufactories, mad-houses, lazarettos,
hospitals, and schools: with a plan of management adapted
to the principle." See also the elegant charts and diagrams
in Julius, *op. cit.*, vol. II.

[148]"In the centre was written the name Jeliabov. It
was circled in red. From this circle lines extended to
other but smaller circles. These in turn were centres of
other lines that extended to other circles, and so on.
The result was that direct and indirect contacts of the
terrorist [Jeliabov] could be immediately grasped. The
red circles represented Jeliabov's political contacts: there
were 34 of them; the yellow ones represented his relatives
(10); the green circles indicated his friends and non-
political acquaintances (17). The brown circles, numbering
327, represented people who, for various reasons, were in
contact with any of the others. There was one for lawyer,
Jrigoni, (red circle) who had relatives in Odessa (6 brown
circles) of whom an uncle also belonged to the [terrorist
organization] Narodnaia Volia but who did not know
Jeliabov personally. Other signs indicated that the
terrorist had purely friendly relations with the student
Barenski (green circle) who knew 16 people in St. Peters-
burg, 3 in Kiev, 4 in Moscow, etc. Presumably Jeliabov
knew nothing of them; thus the police knew his particulars
better than he did himself." Maurice Laporte, *Histoire
de l'Okhrana: la police secrète des Tsars, 1880-1917*,
(Paris, Payot, 1935), 39-40.

[149]*Discipline and Punish*, 184.

[150]*Discipline and Punish*, 225.

[151]*Discipline and Punish*, 271.

[152]Foucault, "Entretien sur la prison: le livre et sa méthode" *Magazine littéraire,* 101 (juin, 1975), 29.

[153]A directly analogous service is provided by the *blatnye* in the camps of the GULag.

[154]Foucault, "Entretien sur la prison," 31. Or, more bluntly: "The more delinquents there are, the more the population accepts police controls." Foucault, "Entretien: Des supplices aux cellules," *Le Monde,* (21 fév., 1975), 17. Hence the importance of "crime waves" generated by obliging police statisticians.

[155]"Résumé de cours," 167.

[156]Katia D. Kaupp and Franz-Olivier Giesbert, "Les prisons de Pleven," *Le Nouvel Observateur,* 375 (17 jan. 1972), 24-26. In 1972 two new groups, The Association for the Defence of Prisoners' Rights, and the Prisoners Action Group, were formed from the G.I.P. See *Le Monde,* (6 déc., 1972), 20.

[157]*Enquête dans une prison-modèle: Fleury-Mérogis,* (Paris, Editions Champ Libre, 1971), back cover.

[158]"Revolutionary Action: 'Until Now,'" in *Language, Counter-Memory, Practice,* 227.

[159]Foucault, "Préface," to Livrozet, *De la prison à la revolte: Essai-témoinage,* (Paris, Mercure de France, 1973), 8.

[160]For details, see Maurice Clavel, "Un manifestant bien élevé," *Le Nouvel Observateur,* 424 (23 déc., 1972), 56; *Le Monde,* (28-29 juillet, 1974), 8; Foucault, "Préface" to Bernard Cuau, *L'Affaire Mirval, ou comment le recit abolit le crime,* (Paris, Les Presses d'Aujourd'hui, 1976); Foucault, "Va-t-on extrader Klaus Croissant?" *Le Nouvel Observateur,* 679 (14 nov., 1977), 62-3; Foucault, "Préface," to Mireille Debard and Jean-Luc Henning, *Les Juges kaki,* (Paris, Moreau, 1977).

[161]"Intellectuals and Power," in *Language, Counter-Memory, Practice,* 210.

[162]Foucault, "Les Deux morts de Pompidou," *Le Nouvel Observateur*, 421 (4 déc., 1972), 56.

[163]These are what Jean Baechler, in his exhaustive account of the phenomenon of self-destruction, called "suicides of flight." They are, under some circumstances, completely intelligible and rational responses to a situation experienced as intolerable. See Baechler, *Suicides*, tr. B. Cooper, (New York, Basic Books, 1979), Ch. 3.

[164]*Ibid.*, 57.

[165]"Revolutionary Action: 'Until Now'," in *Language, Counter-Memory, Practice*, 230.

[166]See the very amusing exchange of letters between Foucault and Amié Pastre, *Le Nouvel Observateur*, 422 (11 déc., 1972), 63.

[167]Foucault, "Manières de justice," *Le Nouvel Observateur*, 743, (5 fév., 1979), 20-1.

[168]Foucault, Jean Laplanche, Robert Badinter "L'Angoisse de juger," *Le Nouvel Observateur*, 655 (30 mai, 1977), 120.

[169]Foucault, "Du bon usage du criminel," *Le Nouvel Observateur*, 722, (11 sept., 1978), 42. The danger of relying on confessions rather than proving the crime is not confined to France. See, for example, the account of a similar event in *The Sunday Times*, (10 Aug. 1980), 31.

[170]Foucault's other positive actions were centred on establishing the philosophy faculty at Vincennes. Within two years of its establishment the Minister of Education, Olivier Guichard, refused to grant graduates their *licence* because, he said, they studied Marxism and politics, not philosophy. Ten years later, it has disappeared—or rather, has been moved to a much smaller space in a working-class part of Paris. See the interview with Foucault, *Le Nouvel Observateur*, 274 (9 fév., 1970), 33-35. Foucault has also spoken of "political spirituality" as an alternative to the existing order (see Perrot, ed., *L'Impossible Prison, op. cit.*, 51) and of a novel "political will" in connection with Iran (see Foucault, "A quoi rêvent les Iraniens?" *Le Nouvel Observateur*, 727 (16 oct., 1978), 48-49; see also Foucault, "Lettre ouvert à Mehdi Bazargan," *Ibid.*, 753 (14 avril, 1979), 46,

and "L'esprit d'un monde sans esprit," in Claude Brière and Pierre Blanchet, *Iran: la Révolution au nom de Dieu,* (Paris, Deuil, 1979), 225-41. No doubt he meant something by terms such as political spirituality, but his remarks were too sketchy to allow for any elaboration. Finally, he has provided some financial and editorial support for the radical (and very funny) newspaper, *Libération.*

[171]Foucault, "Sur la justice poplaire: débat avec les Maos," *Les Temps modernes,* 310 *bis* (1972), 339.

[172]An eloquent and wide-ranging text is Otto Kirch-heimer, *Political Justice: The Use of Legal Procedure for Political Ends,* (Princeton, Princton University Press, 1961).

[173]Foucault, "Sur la justice populaire," 354.

[174]Foucault, "Résumé des cours et traveaux," Collège de France, *Annuaire,* (Paris, Imprimerie de Palais Royal, 1978), 445.

[175]*Ibid,* 446.

[176]See Jacques Donzelot, "Espace clos: travail et moralisation," *Topique,* 3 (mai, 1970), 125-152.

[177]Foucault, "Résumé des cours," 446.

[178]*Loc. cit.*

[179]*Ibid.,* 447.

[180]*Ibid.,* 448. See also Foucault, "La Stratégie du partour," *Le Nouvel Observateur,* 759 (28 mai, 1979), 57.

[181]Foucault, *The History of Sexuality,* vol. I, *An Introduction,* trans. Robert Hurley, (New York, Pantheon, 1968), 136.

[182]*Ibid.,* 137.

[183]*Ibid.,* 144.

[184]Foucault, "Résumé des cours et traveaux," College de France, *Annuaire*, (Paris, Imprimerie de Palais Royal, 1976), 363.

[185]*Ibid*., 364.

[186](Paris, Michel Brunet, 1722-1738), four vols. There is relatively little secondary or interpretative literature on La Mare's *Traité*; thus the present summary. See, however, Jacques Saint-Germaine, *La Regnie et la police au grand siècle*, (Paris, P.U.F., 1964), Chap. 3; Marc Chassaigne, *La Lieutenance générale de Police de Paris*, (Geneva, Slatkine-Megariotis Reprints, 1975). There is also an extensive correspondence of La Mare in the Bibliothèque Nationale, Paris.

[187]*Traité*, vol. I (1722), 2, 4.

[188]*Ibid*., 4.

[189]*Ibid*., 268.

[190]"Here is the very depth of iniquity and the last source of the heart's corruption. A man who has been weakened or ruined by excesses of luxury, the attractions of gaming, of debauch, or other voluptuous pastimes, and hardened by blasphemy, whether express or tacit, that ordinarily accompanies this state, now will have recourse to diabolic arts, believing to find there what would satisfy his passions or salve his hurts." *Ibid*., 520.

[191]*Ibid*., 534. Book V, published as vol. II (1710) and III (1719) covered "provisioning" and dealt with regulation of grain, animals, wood and charcoal, bread-making, venison, game, pork, butter, eggs, fish, oysters, crab, salt merchants, transport, public markets, herbs, roots, fruits, gardens, seasonings, spices, vinegar, wines, liquors, and hay. Book VI (vol. IV, 1738) dealt with public roadways, buildings, bridges, fire hazards, street paving and cleaning, floods, public access to streets, decoration of cities, and a description and history of Paris (with maps).

[192]Foucault, "L'Oeil du pouvoir," in Jeremy Bentham, *Le Panoptique*, (Paris, Belfond, 1977), 18.

[193] Foucault, "Entretien," *Pro Justitia*, I (1973), 9.

[194] Foucault, "L'Oeil du pouvoir," 24-25. One should add to the list of regularizing agencies political parties, especially left-wing ones. For France see Michèle Manceaux and Jacques Donzelot, *Cours, camrade, le P.C.F. est derrière toi*, (Paris, Gallimard, 1974).

[195] Foucault, *History of Sexuality*, 92.

[196] See Jean Meyer, "Une enquête de l'Académie de Médicine sur les épidemies," *Annales E.S.C.*, 21 (1966), and J-P Peter, "Malades et maladies à la fin du SVIIIe siècle, 729-49, *ibid.*, 22 (1967), 711-51.

[197] Often the genuinely historical spaces of cities have been simply allowed to decline into slums. Then they could be torn down and more efficient use made of the area; alternatively, fashion and market pressures might transform a historical slum into something trendy and desirable. The same process is at work in Le Marais and Cabbagetown, in the XIIIe arrondisement and the West End of Vancouver.

[198] Francois Beguin, "Savoirs de la ville et de la maison au début du 19ème siècle," in M. Foucault, director, Collège de France, Equipe de Recherches de la Chaire d'Histoire des Systèmes de Pensée, *Politiques de l'habitat*, (Paris, CORDA, 1977), 318.

[199] Jean-Marie Alliaume, "Anatomie des discours de reforme," in Foucault, dir., *Politique de l'habitat*, 181.

[200] Danielle Rancière, "La loi du 13 juillet 1830 sur les logements insallubres: les philanthropes et le problème insoluble de l'habitat du pauvre," in Foucault, dir., *Politique de l'habitat*, 199. See also Bruno Fortier, ed., *La Politique de l'espace parisien*, (Paris, CORDA, 1975).

[201] *Ibid.*, 202.

[202] Le Cler du Brillet, "Eloge" in La Mare, *Traité de Police*, vol. IV (1738), xiv.

[203]Michel Foucault, "La Politique de la santé au XVIIIe siècle," in Foucault, ed., *Les Machines à guérir*, (Paris, Institut de l'Environment, 1976), 13.

[204]*Ibid.*, 18.

[205]*Ibid.*, 16.   See also Foucault, "L'Institution hospitalière au XVIIIe siècle," in Foucault, ed., *Généologie des equipements de normalisation: Les equipements sanitaires*, (Paris CERFI, 1976).

[206]Jacques Donzelot, *The Policing of Families*, trans. Robert Hurley, (New York, Pantheon, 1979), 44.

[207]For further details see Philippe Meyer and Jacques Donzelot, *Enfance irregulière et politique familiale: Enquête sur le jurisdictions pour enfants et l'education surveillée*, (Paris, G.E.F.S., 1973).

[208]Foucault, "Résumé de cours," Collège de France, *Annuaire*, (Paris, Imprimerie Palais Royale, 1975), 336.

[209]*Ibid.*, 338.

[210]The directly political implications of a theory of degeneracy were not simply racist.   It is true, of course, that aristocratic racists such as de Gobineau made much of the slaughter of blue-blooded Germanic stock and their replacement with inferior Gauls, but the bourgeoisie had its own (still popular) myth, centred on vampires.   The aristocratic vampire needed the blood of the bourgeoisie to survive; inevitably he was killed by a bourgeois, often with the aid of a priest and the police.   Less arcane was the bourgeois racism of expansion: instead of looking to the past, to an illustrious bloodline, the bourgeois looked to the future, to the production of healthy children.   And lastly there is the Marxist fallout filtered through the concept of a degenerate (bourgeois) class and its healthy classless successor.   See Foucault, *The History of Sexuality*, 124ff., and "Entrevue," *Ornicar?*   88-89.

[211]There is the additional continuity from abnormality, namely abnormal sex. Foucault has edited the memoirs of an hermaphrodite, *Hercule Barbin, dite Alexina B: Mes souvenirs*, (Paris, Gallimard, 1978) in a collection called "Parallel Lives," a kind of counter-Plutarch, the object of which was not to produce illustrious examples but the obscure darkness of life. He also edited a translation of *My Secret Life*, (Paris, Editions les formes du secret, 1977) whose anonymous author, he said, was a kind of counter-Freud. Freud dealt with the sexuality of the psyche and its pains; this "other Victorian" celebrated the sexuality of the body and its pleasures. He also took part in the controversy surrounding the publication of Pierre Guyotat's erotic book *Eden, Eden, Eden*, (Paris, Gallimard, 1970). Guyotat's book was prohibited by the Minister of the Interior for sale to anyone under 18 years. It was not submitted to the commission that usually decided such matters but was simply banned. There followed a well publicized petition with illustrious names at its head. The whole tale is documented in another book by Guyotat, *Littérature interdite* (Paris, Gallimard, 1972). See Foucault, "Il y aura scandale, mais . . . ." *Le Nouvel Observateur*, 304 (7 sept., 1970), 40.

[212]Foucault, "Entretien," *La Quinzaine littéraire*, 247 (11 juin, 1977), 5.

[213]Voltaire, who surely enjoyed the absurdities of spiritualized flesh, told the story of a Jesuit who assigned penance of one rosary for every four fornications; then, when hearing a confession of eleven fornications, told the penitent to have one more go and then say three rosaries.

[214]Foucault, *History of Sexuality*, 8.

[215]*Ibid.*, 32.

[216]*Ibid.*, 35.

[217]*Ibid.*, 44-45.

[218]*Ibid.*, 47

[219]The contrast between a hermeneutic of reminiscence and participation as opposed to one of demystification or disenchantment is borrowed from Paul Ricoeur, *Freud and Philosophy*, trans., D. Savage, (Newhaven, Yale University Press, 1970). I have discussed this question at greater

length elsewhere. For details see "Reason and Interpretation
in Contemporary Political Theory," *Polity* XI (1979), 387-99;
"Hermeneutics and Political Science," in H. K. Betz, ed.,
Recent Approaches to the Social Sciences, vol. II, (Social
Sciences Symposium Series, University of Calgary, 1979),
17-30; "Reduction, Reminiscence and the Search for Truth,"
in Peter Opitz and Gregor Sebba, eds., *Philosophy of Order*,
(Munich, Klett-Kotta, 1980), 179-94.

[220] Foucault, *History of Sexuality*, 61.

[221] This is why Foucault's discourse on sexuality has
not met with universal approval by women and homosexuals
(of either gender) even though, in principle, he certainly
is in favour of "liberation." See the interview with
B.-H. Lévy, "Foucault: Non au sexe roi," *Le Nouvel
Observateur*, 644 (12 mars, 1977), 95-100.

[222] Foucault, *History of Sexuality*, 103.

[223] The hystericization of women by male doctors, which
expressed their fascinations and fear of women's bodies as
well as their desire to dominate and control them, is
discussed in Jean-Pierre Peter, "Entre femmes et medicins,"
Ethnologie francaise, N.S. 6 (1976), 341-48.

[224] *Language, Counter-Memory, Practice*, 171.

[225] Jacques Donzelot, "Misère de la culture politique,"
Critique, 373-74.(1978), 575.

[226] Foucault, "La grande colere des faits," *Le Nouvel
Observateur*, 652 (9 mai, 1977), 85.

[227] Foucault, "La fonction politique de l'intellectuel,"
Politique hebdo, 247 (29 nov., 1976), 33.

BIBLIOGRAPHY

Note: Other bibliographies providing fuller bibliographical accounts of Foucault's work (translations into German, Italian, etc.) and a selection of secondary literature and commentary are: Francois H. Lapointe and Claire Lapointe, "Bibliographia," *Dialogos* 10:26 (1974) 153-57; *idem.*, *Dialogos* 11:29-30 (1977), 245-54; Christian Jambet, "Bibliographie," *Magazine littéraire* 101 (juin, 1975), 24-26; W. Seitter, "Bibliographie des Schriften Michel Foucaults," in W. Seitter, ed., *Michel Foucault, Von der Subversion des Wissens*. Munich, Piper, 1974. There is also a bibliography appended to Alan Sheridan *Michel Foucault, The Will to Truth*. London, Tavistock, 1980 and to Colin Gordon, ed., *Power/Knowledge: Selected Interviews and Other Writings, 1972-1977*. New York, Pantheon, 1980. The present bibliography includes only works in French or in English translations. I have not been able to verify all entries.

1954

Maladie mentale et psychologie, Paris, P.U.F. (new ed. 1966). Trans. Alan Sheridan, *Mental Illness and Psychology*. New York, Harper, 1976.

Introduction to L. Binswanger, *Le Rêve et l'existence*. Desclée de Brouwer.

1957

"La Recherche du psychologue," in *Des Chercheurs francais s'interrogent*. Paris.

1958

Translator. Viktor von Weizsaecker, *Le Cycle de la Structure [Der Gestaltkreis]*, with Daniel Rocher. Bruges, Desclée de Brouwer, 1958.

1961

*Folie et déraison: Histoire de la folie à l'âge
classique.* Paris, Plon. New, enlarged ed. Gallimard,
1972. Trans. R. Howard, *Madness and Civilization:
A History of Insanity in the Age of Reason.* New York,
Pantheon, 1965.

"Entretien: La folie n'existe que dans une société,"
Le Monde (22 juillet), 9.

Review, A. Koyré *Etudes newtoniennes, NRF* 108, 123-24.

1962

Introduction to *Rousseau, Juge de Jean-Jacques.*
Paris, Colin.

"Dire et voir chez Raymond Roussel," *Lettre ouverte,*
été, no. 4, 38-51.

Translator, "Art du Langage et linguistique," in
Leo Spitzer, *Etudes de Style.* Paris, Gallimard.

"Le cycle de grenouilles," *NRF*, 114, 1159-65.

"Le 'non' du père," *Critique*, 178, 195-209.

"Un si cruel savoir," *Critique*, 182, 597-611.

1963

*Naissance de la clinique: Un archéologie du regard
médical.* Paris, P.U.F. Trans. A. M. Sheridan
Smith, *The Birth of the Clinic: An Archeology of
Medical Perception.* New York, Vintage, 1975.

Raymond Roussel, Paris, Gallimard.

"La métamorphose et le labyrinthe," *NRF*, 124, avril.

"Préface à la transgression," *Critique*, 195-96, 761-69.

"Guetter le jour qui vient," *NRF*, 130, oct., 709-16.

"Distance, aspect, origine," *Critique*, 198, 931-45.

"Le langage à l'infini," *Tel Quel* 15, août, 44-53.

1964

Translation. Kant, *Anthropologie du point du vue pragmatique*. Paris, Vrin.

"La prose d' Actéon," *NRF* 135, 444-59.

"Le langage de l'espace," *Critique* 203, avril, 378-82.

"Le Mallarmé de [J.-P.] Richard," *Annales*, sept.-oct. 996-1004.

"Débat sur le roman," *Tel Quel*, 17, printemps, 12-54.

"Debat sur la poesie," *ibid*.

"Nerval, est-il le plus grand poète du XIXe siècle?" *Arts*, 11 nov.

"Pourquoi réédite-t-on Raymond Roussel? Un précurseur de notre littérature moderne," *Le Monde*, 22 aout, 9.

"La folie, l'absence d'oeuvre," *La Table ronde*, mai.

1966

Les mots et les choses. Paris, Gallimard. Trans. *The Order of Things: An Archeology of the Human Sciences*. Trans. Anon. London, Tavistock Publications, 1970.

"L'Arrière-Fable," *L'Arc*, 29, 5-12.

"La Pensée du dehors," *Critique 229, juin, 523-46*.

"Entretien avec Madeleine Chapsal," *La Quinzaire littéraire*, 15 mai.

"Entretien avec Raymond Bellour," *Les lettres francaises* 1125, mars 31, 3-4.

"Entretien avec Claude Bonnefoy," *Arts et Loisirs* 38, 15 juin, 8-9.

"La Prose du monde," *Diogènes*, 53.

"Une Histoire restée muette," *La Quinzaine littéraire*, 8.

"Entretien avec Claude Bonnefoy," *Arts et Loisirs* 54, 5 octobre.

1967

Intro. [with Gilles Deleuze] F. W. Nietzsche,
Le Gai Savoir, Paris, Gallimard.

"Nietzsche, Freud, Marx," *Cahiers de Royaumont*, 7.

"Un 'fantastique' de bibliothèque," *Cahiers de la
Compagnie Renaud-Barrault*, 59, mars, 7-30.

"Deuxième entretien avec Raymond Bellour," *Les lettres
francaises*, 1187, juin 15, 6-9.

"Les mots et les images," *Le Nouvel Observateur*, 154,
25 oct., 49-50.

"Entretien: la publication des *Oeuvres complètes* de
Nietzsche," *Le Monde*, 24 mai, p. viii.

"La grammaire générale de Port-Royal," *Langages*, 7.

1968

"Réponse à une question," *Esprit*, 371, mai, 850-74.

"Réponse au cercle d'épistémologie," *Cahiers pour
l'analyse*, 9, été, 9-40.

"Les déviations religieuses et le savoir médical,"
in J. LeGoff, ed., *Herésie et sociétés*. Paris - The
Hague, Mouton.

"Correspondance" *La Pensée*, 139.

1969

L'Archéologie du savoir. Paris, Gallimard. Trans.
A. M. Sheridan Smith, *The Archeology of Knowledge*.
New York, Harper, 1976.

Introduction to Arnauld and Lancelot, *Grammaire
générale et raisonée*. Paris, Paulet.

"Qu'est-ce qu'un auteur?" Conference, 22 avril, Société
francaise de philosophie. *Bulletin de la Société
francaise de philosophie*, LXIV (1970) 73-104.

"Ariane s'est pendue," *Le Nouvel Observateur*, 229,
31 mars.

Paulo Caruso, *Conversazioni con Claude Lévi-Strauss, Michel Foucault, Jacques Lacan.* Milano. Mursia.

"Foucault répond à Sartre," *La Quinzaine littéraire,* 1 mars, 20-22.

"Entretien" *Magazine littéraire,* 28, avril-mai, 23-25.

"Jean Hyppolite (1907-1968)," *Revue de métaphysique et de morale,* 74, 131-36.

"La naissance d'un monde" *Le Monde,* 3 mai.

1970

Introduction to Georges Bataille, *Oeuvres complètes.* Paris, Gallimard.

"Sept propos sur la septième ange," in J. P. Brisset, ed., *La grammaire logique.* Paris, Tchou.

"Theatrum philosophicum," *Critique* 282, nov., 885-908.

"Il y aura scandale, mais . . . ." *La Nouvel Observateur,* 304, 7 sept., 40.

"La bibliotheque fantastique," in R. Debray-Genette, ed., *Flaubert: Miroir de la critique.* Paris, Payot.

"La Logique du Vivant," *Le Monde* 15-16 novembre, p. 13.

"La Situation de Cuvier dans l'histoire de la biologie," *Revue d'histoire des sciences et de leurs applications,* 23.

"La piège de Vincennes," *Le nouvel observateur* 274 (9 fev.).

1971

L'Ordre du discours. Paris, Gallimard.

Introduction to G. Flaubert, *La Tentation de saint Antoine.* Paris, Livre de Poche.

"Nietzsche, la généologie, l'histoire," in *Hommage à Jean Hyppolite,* ed. Foucault. Paris, P.U.F.

"Résumés des cours et traveaux," Collège de France, *Annuaire*. Paris, Presses du Palais Royal, 245-46.

"A Conversation with Michel Foucault," *Partisan Review* 38, 192-201.

"Entretiens" in Raymound Bellour, *Le Livre des autres*. Paris, Herne. (Reprinted from *Les lettres francaises*, 1966-67.)

"Entretien" with M.-A. Burnier and Philippe Graine, *Actuel* 14 (nov.). Reprinted in M. Foucault *et al., C'est Demain la veille*. Paris, Seuil, 1973.

"Monstrosities in Criticism," *Diacritics*, 1.

"Foucault Responds," *Diacritics* I:2 winter, 60.

"Le Discours de Toul," *Le Nouvel Observateur* 372 (27 déc.).

1972

"Bachelard, le philosphe et son ombre," *Le Figaro littéraire*, 1376, 30 avril.

"History, Discourse, and Discontinuity," *Salmagundi* 20, summer-fall, 225-48.

"Les intellectuels et le pouvoir," *L'Arc*, 49.

"Sur la justice populaire: Débat avec les maos," *Les Temps modernes*, 310 *bis*, 335-66.

"Les deux morts de Pompidou," *Le Nouvel Observateur* 421, 4 déc., 56-57.

"Correspondance," *Le Nouvel Observateur*, 422, 11 déc., 63.

"Résumés des cours et traveaux," Collège de France, *Annuaire*, Paris, Presses du Palais Royal, 283-86.

"Piéger sa propre culture" *Le Figaro*, (30 sept.).

"Medecine et lutte de classe" *La Nef* 49.

"Table rounde," *Exprit*, special issue (avril-mai).

1973

Ceci n'est pas une pipe. Montpellier, Fata Morgana.

Introduction to Serge Livrozet, *De la Prison à la révolte.* Paris, Mercure de France.

"Entretien" in Foucault, H. Lefebvre, H. Marcuse, *et al., C'est demain la veille.* Paris, Seuil.

Moi, Pierre Rivière, ayant égorgé ma mere, ma soeur et mon frère . . . . Paris, Gallimard-Juillard. Trans. F. Hellinek, *I, Pierre Rivière, having slaughtered my mother, my sister, and my brother* . . . . New York, Pantheon, 1975.

"Résumés des cours et traveaux," Collège de France, *Annuaire*: Paris, Presses du Palais Royal, 255-67.

"Entretien" *Pro Justitia* I:3-4, 5-14.

"La Force de fuir" in P. Rebeyrolle, *Derrière le mirror.* Paris.

"En guise de conclusion," *Le Nouvel Observateur,* 435, (13 mars).

"Convoqués à la P. J." *Le Nouvel Observateur,* 468 (29 oct.).

"Pour une chronique de la mémoire ouvrière," *Libération* 22 fév.

1974

"Entretien avec R. P. Droit," *Monde des livres,* 21 fév.

"Résumés des cours et traveaux," Collège de France, *Annuaire.* Paris, Presses du Palais Royal, 293-300.

"Anti-rétro," *Cahiers du Cinema,* 251-2, juillet-août.

"Preface" to B. Jackson, *Leurs Prisons* Paris, G.I.P.

"Les rayons noirs de Byzantios," *Le Nouvel Observateur,* 483 (11 fév.).

"On Attica," *Telos* 19, spring.

1975

Surveiller et punir. Paris, Gallimard. Trans. Alan
Sheridan. *Discipline and Punish.* New York,
Pantheon, 1977.

"La peinture photogenique," catalogue for Gérard
Fromanger, *Le désir est partout.* Paris, Galerie
Jeanne Bucher.

"Résumés des cours et traveaux," Collège de France,
Annuaire. Paris, Presses du Palais Royal, 335-39.

"Entretien sur la prison: le livre et sa méthode,"
Magazine littéraire, 101 (juin), 27-33.

"Entretien: Des supplices aux cellules," *Le Monde,*
21 fév., pp.16-17.

"Un pompier vend la meche" *Le Nouvel Observateur,*
531 (13 jan.).

"Entretien," *Les nouvelles littéraires,* 17 mars.

"Pouvoir et corps," *Quel Corps?* 2 (sept.-oct.).

1976

"Résumés des cours et traveaux," Collège de France,
Annuaire. Paris, Presses du Palais Royal, 361-66.

"La politique de la santé au XVIIIe siècle," in M.
Foucault, *et al., Les Machines à guérir.* Paris,
Institut de l'environnement, 11-21.

"Preface" to Bernard Ciran, *L'Affaire Mirval, ou
comment le récit abolit le crime.* Paris, Les Presses
d'Aujourd'hui.

"Preface" to Wiaz, *En attendant le grand soir.*
Paris, Denöel.

Histoire de la sexualite, vol. I, *La volunté de savoir.*
Paris, Gallimard. Trans. Robert Hurley, *The History
of Sexuality,* vol. I, *An Introduction.* New York,
Pantheon, 1978.

"L'Occident et la vérité du sexe," *Le Monde,* 5 nov.,
p.24.

"La fonction politique de l'intellectuel,"
Politique hebdo 247 (29 nov.), 31-3.

"L'Institution hospitalière au XVIIIe siècle,"
*Généologie des équipments de normalisation: Les
equipements sanitaires.* Paris, CERFI. 1-79.

"Questions à Michel Foucault sur la géographie"
Hérodote, 1, jan.-mars.

"Crimés et châtiments en URSS et ailleurs,"
Le nouvel observateur, 585, 26 jan.

"Malreaux," *Le Nouvel Observateur*, 629, 29 nov., 83.

"Sorcellerie et folie," *Le Monde*, 23 avril.

"Des reponses aux questions" *Herodote*, 4, oct-déc.

1977

"Résumés des cours et traveaux," Collège de France,
Annuaire. Paris, Presses du Palais Royal, 445-49.

"Entretien" *Le Nouvel Observateur*, 644, 12 mars, 92-130.

"Va-t-on extrader Klaus Croissant?" *Le Nouvel
Observateur*, 679, 14 nov., 62-63.

"L'angoisse de juger," *Le Nouvel Observateur*, 655,
30 mai, 92-126.

"L'asile illimité," *Le Nouvel Observateur*, 646, 28
mars, 66-67.

"La grande colère des faits," *Le Nouvel Observateur*,
652, 9 mai, 84-86.

"Entretien" *La Quinzaine littéraire*, 247, 1 jan., 4-6.

"Pouvoirs et stratégies," *Les Révoltes logiques*,
4, 89-97.

"Enferment, psychiatrie, prison," *Change*, 32-33,
76-110.

"Preface" to Mireille Debard and Jean-Luc Henning,
Les Juges kaki. Paris, Moreau, 7-10.

Director, J. M. Alliaume *et al., Politiques de l'habitat:
1800-1850.* Paris, CORDA.

"L'oeil du pouvoir" in Jeremy Bentham, *Le Panoptique.*
Paris, Belfond, 9-31.

Préface to trans. of *My Secret Life.* Paris,
Editions des formes du secret.

*Language, Counter-Memory, and Practice: Selected
Essays and Interviews,* ed. D. F. Bouchard, trans.
D. F. Bouchard and S. Simon. Ithaca, Cornell
University Press.

"Entrevue: le jeu de Michel Foucault," *"Ornicar?*
(1977) 62-93.

"Preface" to English translation of G. Deleuze and
F. Fuattari, *Anti-Oedipus.* New York, Random House.

"La vie des hommes infâmes" in *Les Cahiers du
Chemin.* Paris.

"Entretien," *Le Matin,* 18 nov.

1978

"Du bon usage du criminel," *Le Nouvel Observateur,*
722, 11 sept., 40-42.

"A quoi rêvent les Iraniens?" *Le Nouvel Observateur,*
727, 16 oct., 48-49.

Editor, *Hercule Barbin, dite Alexina B. (Mes
Souvenirs).* Paris, Gallimard. Trans. Richard
McDougal, *Herculine Barbin: Being the Recently
Discovered Memoirs of a Nineteenth-Century French
Hermaphrodite.* New York, Pantheon, 1980.

"Le citron et le lait" *Le Monde,* (21-2 oct.).

"Des hommes qui ne voulaient pas devenir des fauves,"
Libération, (22 mars).

Articles on Iran, *Corriera della Sera* (Milan) (5 nov.;
7 nov.; 19 nov.; 26 nov.).

"Table ronde sur l'expertise psychiatrique," in
Delinquances et ordre. Paris.

1979

"Manières de justice," *Le Nouvel Observateur*, 743,
5 fév., 20-21.

"Pour une morale de l'inconfort," *Le Nouvel
Observateur*, 754, 23 avril, 82-83.

"Lettre ouvert a Mehdi Bazargan," *Le Nouvel
Observateur*, 753, 14 avril, 46.

"La stratégie du pouvoir," *Le Nouvel Observateur*,
759, 28 mai, 57.

"Vivre autrement le temps," *Le Nouvel Observateur*,
755, 30 avril, 88.

"L'esprit d'un monde sans esprit," in Claire Brière
Pierre Blanchet, *Iran: la révolution au nom de Dieu.*
Paris, Seuil, 225-41.

"Preface" to Pierre Brückner, *Ennemi de l'Etat,*
Paris.

"Un plaisir si simple," *Le Gai Pied*, 1 (avril).

"Inutile de se soulever" *Le Monde*, (11-12 mai).

1980

Michelle Perrot, Michel Foucault, *et al.*, *L'Impossible
Prison: Recherches sur le systeme peniteniare aux XIX*e
siecle: Débat avec Michel Foucault. Paris, Seuil.

*Power/Knowledge: Selected Interviews and Other
Writings, 1972-1977, by Michel Foucault.* Ed., Colin
Gordon. New York, Pantheon.

INDEX

STUDIES IN RELIGION AND SOCIETY

Barry Cooper is professor of political science at the University of Calgary. He has translated works by Jean Baechler and Raymond Aron and has published an number of articles in political science and Canadian politics. **Merleau-Ponty and Marxism: From Terror to Reform** is a recent major work and **The End of History: An Essay in French Hegelianism** is a forthcoming book from the University of Toronto Press.